The
Paraprofessional's Handbook for
Effective Support in
Inclusive Classrooms

The
Paraprofessional's Handbook for Effective Support in Inclusive Classrooms

by

Julie Causton-Theoharis, Ph.D.
Syracuse University
New York

Baltimore • London • Sydney

Paul H. Brookes Publishing Co.
Post Office Box 10624
Baltimore, Maryland 21285-0624
USA

www.brookespublishing.com

"Paul H. Brookes Publishing Co." is a registered trademark
of Paul H. Brookes Publishing Co., Inc.

Typeset by Broad Books, Baltimore, Maryland.
Manufactured in the United States of America by
Sheridan Books, Inc., Chelsea, Michigan.

Some of the individuals described in this book are composites whose
situations are masked and are based on the author's experiences. In some
cases, permission has been granted to use actual names; in other cases,
names and identifying details have been changed to protect confidentiality.

The cartoons that appear on pages 1, 11, 27, 39, 51, 61, 75, 95, and 101
are reprinted with permission from Giangreco, M.F. (2007). *Absurdities
and realities of special education: The complete digital set* [CD]. Thousand
Oaks, CA: Corwin Press.

Library of Congress Cataloging-in-Publication Data
Causton-Theoharis, Julie.
    The paraprofessional's handbook for effective support in inclusive
    classrooms / Julie Causton-Theoharis.
          p.   cm.
    Includes bibliographical references and index.
    ISBN-13: 978-1-55766-899-8 (pbk.)
    ISBN-10: 1-55766-899-X
    1. Inclusive education—Handbooks, manuals, etc.   2. Children with disabilities—
    Education—Handbooks, manuals, etc.   3. Children with disabilities—Services for—
    Handbooks, manuals, etc.   4. Teachers' assistants—Handbooks, manuals, etc.   I. Title.
    LC1200.C38   2009
    371.9´046–dc22   2009011459

British Library Cataloguing in Publication data are available from the British Library.

2019

10   9

Contents

About the Author vii

Foreword   *Paula Kluth* ix

Preface xiii

Acknowledgments xvii

1   The Paraprofessional 1

2   Special Education 11

3   Inclusive Education 27

4   Collaborating with Others: Working within a Team 39

5   Rethinking Students: Presuming Competence 51

6   Providing Social Supports: Standing Back 61

7   Providing Academic Supports 75

    Appendix   Useful Web Sites and

    Resources for Assistive Technology 93

8   Providing Behavioral Supports 95

9   Supporting You Supporting Them: Self-Care 111

    Appendix   Resources for Paraprofessionals 119

References 121

Index 125

About the Author

Julie Causton-Theoharis, Ph.D., is a professor in the Inclusive Special Education Program at Syracuse University. She teaches courses on inclusion, differentiation, adaptations, and collaboration. Her published works have appeared in such journals as *Exceptional Children, TEACHING Exceptional Children, Journal of Research in Childhood Education, International Journal of Inclusive Education, Behavioral Disorders, Studies in Art Education,* and *Equity and Excellence in Education.* Dr. Causton-Theoharis also works as an educational consultant in schools and districts nationwide.

Foreword

When I was hired for my first teaching job—the inclusion facilitator for a school just launching an inclusive model—I looked forward to planning curriculum and instruction, developing lesson plans, collaborating with general educators, designing learning environments, and creating learning materials. I envisioned spending most of my time coteaching, providing support to students with and without disabilities, and making curricular adaptations.

When school started on my first day of teaching, that vision quickly evaporated. After escorting one student off the bus, Jo, one of the paraprofessionals assigned to my team, approached me to ask, "Where am I supposed to be?" I told her to ask the principal. She had asked the principal, she informed me. The principal had told her to ask me! I told Jo to follow me to my office and as we began shuffling through a stack of papers to find student schedules, another paraprofessional, Amy, ran in and screamed, "Byron's screaming and he's on the floor!" I followed Amy out the door with Jo in tow and as we quickly and quietly tried to soothe Byron and help his third-grade teacher restore calm to the classroom, a kindergarten teacher popped her head in to tell me that she had a student with autism under a table in her classroom and couldn't get him out. She wondered when the paraprofessional assigned to her classroom was going to show up.

School started at 9:00 AM, it was now only 9:08 AM, and I was getting a glimpse into life as an inclusion facilitator and as a supervisor and colleague of a whole team of paraprofessionals.

By day's end, I had spent almost every moment not with students, but supporting, directing, and managing the schedules of paraprofessionals! And I can only imagine the perspectives of the eight paraprofessionals, most of them new to the school and to the job in general. They must have felt like novice sailors on a sinking ship. I doubt that having a captain with several hours of experience was any comfort.

Things could only have gotten better, however, and they did. I was stunned to learn about the many responsibilities I would have with the team of paraprofessionals. At first I balked at some of these duties, including holding team meetings, writing out and explaining procedures for student health needs and behaviors, and supervising women who had far more experience with children than I did.

Eventually, however, life with this big team fell into a comfortable rhythm and I learned that having so many paraprofessionals on the team was not only teaching me about collaboration and team building, but also was offering this first-year teacher much-needed support, encouragement, and inspiration. It was Jo who first encouraged Byron, a student with significant sensory and communication needs, to not only tolerate standing on stage for the holiday concert but to dance and hum along with his peers. It was Amy who convinced a sixth-grade teacher to give her some coteaching responsibilities, thus helping all staff members consider new possibilities for staff collaboration. And it was another paraprofessional, Jeanne, an astute observer and wise person in general, who quietly and calmly came to me daily and reported on all the progress students and staff were making in our fledgling inclusive school. And perhaps the most welcome support came from Ann, who came only in the afternoons and always with some "gift" for the rest of us—home-baked treats, jokes cut from the newspaper, or a toy or gadget that might be used to differentiate instruction for one of our students.

Looking back on my teaching career, I realize that my years on that extended team were great preparation for the rest of my career. So much of my education as a teacher came from the many paraprofessionals on my team. Because of this, I wouldn't change any part of that experience, but I do have one regret: I regret (boy, do I regret) that I didn't have *The Paraprofessional's Handbook for Effective Support in Inclusive Classrooms*. When I received the manuscript and turned the pages, I just kept muttering, marking the pages, and shaking my head. "Yes," I kept thinking, "That's how I should have done it!" "What a great idea!" and "Why didn't I think of that?" This is the book that would have helped my team get off to a smooth start. This is the book that would have given all of our paraprofessionals a foundation and a philosophy for their daily work. This is the book that Jo, Amy, Jeanne, and Ann could have referenced daily for information on behavior, adapting lessons, working with general educators, communicating with students, and facilitating peer relationships. This is the book that would have helped the entire team understand our roles and our responsibilities to one another. This is the book that would have made that first day (and so many after) a bit more peaceful and a lot more organized!

This topic of supporting paraprofessionals has been too long ignored in the literature, in teacher education programs, and even in staff development plans. If you are holding this book, consider yourself lucky because you will not have to "invent the wheel" as many paraprofessionals, teachers, and other related staff members have had to in the past.

Although this book is written primarily for paraprofessionals, it is relevant for many audiences. Whether you are a paraprofessional looking for ways to support students, collaborate, and communicate with team members; a teacher who is seeking ideas for educating and supporting the paraprofessionals on your team; or an administrator needing guidance on how to supervise programs or grow an inclusive school, this book will provide answers, ideas, and many, many "ah ha!" moments.

Julie Causton-Theoharis has carefully designed a text that contains everything the new (or seasoned) paraprofessional needs to know. She explains the "what" and the "why" of inclusive schools and provides information about the law and the philosophies connected to this movement. The book also contains collaboration guidelines and tips; frameworks for describing student behavior and thinking about individual needs; guidance on creating social supports and facilitating friendships; and specific suggestions for addressing certain behaviors, learning needs, and health issues. This information is critical; even today, I meet paraprofessionals who have been given little or no information on these topics.

I want to add that it is not only the rich content of this book that impresses me but the format as well. No staff member is busier than a paraprofessional, so any resources created for this group must be well designed and get-me-ready-for-Monday-morning useful! *The Paraprofessional's Handbook* is just that. This book is full of tables, lists, and formats that are not only user-friendly but instructive. In addition, the chapters are full of stories, some very touching and others funny and oh-so-honest.

In sum, paraprofessionals are too critical to our schools to leave on the margins of our planning, conversations, and training. Julie Causton-Theoharis not only realizes this but communicates it in every page of this smart and well-researched guide.

This is the book I wish I had owned 20 years ago. I am thrilled, that you, reader, have it today.

Paula Kluth, Ph.D.
Oak Park, Illinois

Preface

We are willing and ready to connect with other kids, and adults must quietly step into the background, camouflaging their help as a tiger who may hide
in full view. It's the needed disguise of the adult who smoothes the way for
friendship, then stands back in the shadows, observing the complicated
dance of steps taking you to the feeling of confidence.
> —Jamie Burke, a student with autism, who now attends Syracuse University
> (Tashie, Shapiro-Barnard, & Rossetti, 2008, p. 185)

··········

Then I Met Jill

I had just been hired in the middle of the school year as a special educator to work in
an inclusive fourth-grade classroom. I was to observe that day, before I began my official responsibilities as a teacher. I was introduced to my coteacher, Kathie, and then I
met Jill, the paraprofessional who would be working with me in this classroom. The
bell rang and the students poured in. I was there to learn about the children that day,
but I couldn't help but notice Jill.

Throughout this particular day she settled the students, asked them about
special events, checked off their homework, offered kind words, pointed to page
numbers, helped settle disputes by listening to and talking with the children, set up
partnerships, stepped back when students were being successful, encouraged friendships between a student who did not speak and her peers, wiped tears, found gym
shoes, faded her support beautifully, got a bandage, ran a small reading group, wrote
directions on the board as the teacher gave instructions, read a book aloud, provided
visual cues to kids (very subtly), fixed a student's AlphaSmart communication device,
made copies, and cut out laminating material. Jill managed to do all of this with light-
ning speed and effortless grace . . . and all before lunch!

What I have come to admire most about Jill was not her efficiency, her versa-
tility, or even her energy, but her ability to do what Jamie Burke calls for in the pre-
vious quote. It was her ability to seamlessly support all students in unobtrusive ways.
She has the ability to "camouflage her help" to smooth the way, to stick up for students while simultaneously standing back to allow them to succeed. She not only
created an opportunity for friendships, but also she stepped away from them as soon
as they began interacting in order to allow for natural interaction. She provided

academic support to a few students who needed it, but she supported the whole classroom so it was not evident to others whom she was there to support. This support was so powerful because she allowed these students to be themselves, to interact naturally with others, and to connect socially and academically. At times she provided invisible supports, and at other times she was visible—supporting the entire class. But often it was her light touch, her ability to support and then move on, that impressed me the most.

On Inclusion

Not a day goes by when I don't think about inclusion. When I think of the amazing students I have had the privilege of teaching, I am reminded of what *teachers* they were to me. They have taught me that everyone has a right to belong, to have friends, to have engaging curricula, and to have powerful instruction. Everyone has a right to be treated with dignity and with gentle, respectful support, and to experience that learning is intimately connected with feeling part of the classroom. Every student deserves to receive support in a warm and welcoming place. The more this happens, the more we have created the environment for substantial learning. It isn't, therefore, just about creating a sense of belonging for belonging's sake; that sense of connection and welcome paves the way for academic and social growth. Therefore, this book is designed as a guide for paraprofessionals and other team members as they work to include students with disabilities in gentle and respectful ways.

How This Book Is Organized

The first three chapters provide the context for the rest of the book: Chapter 1 focuses on the role of the paraprofessional, Chapter 2 provides background about special education, and Chapter 3 provides basic information about inclusive education. These first foundational chapters provide the foundation necessary to more effectively interpret the rest of the book and with a framework for situating professional roles within schools and classrooms. Chapter 4 is designed to help paraprofessionals rethink students. In this chapter, I ask paraprofessionals to look at students through the lens of strengths and abilities—to reconsider some of the negative descriptors—for the sake of being able to reach and support all students more effectively. Chapters 5–8 are strategy-specific chapters that focus on collaboration, social supports, academic supports, and behavioral supports. These strategy-specific chapters provide ideas that are immediately applicable in schools. The last chapter focuses on self-care and problem solving. The job of supporting students in our school systems who pose the greatest challenges and require the most complex problem solving is not an easy one. Chapter 9 is meant to give helpful ideas for how paraprofessionals can care for themselves in order to provide the best possible attention for students.

Who Will Find This Book Useful?

As more and more schools move toward inclusive education, paraprofessionals are one of the most critical factors to success because they are on the front lines, making daily decisions that support or deny access to curricula and peers. The idea of the paraprofessional as the linchpin to inclusion disrupts our traditional thinking about inclusion being successful solely because of leaders, curricula, or teachers. Paraprofessionals are equally important partners in the work of doing inclusion well. They need to be valued deeply because they play a key role in the facilitation of learning. Conversely, without appropriate training or support, paraprofessionals can make student success much more difficult—if not impossible. That being said, a team approach to supporting students in the classroom is necessary. Although this book will primarily serve paraprofessionals who want to learn more about supporting students in inclusive classrooms, it is critical that this book is read by the special educators, general educators, administrators, and parents, who are team players in supporting students in inclusive school communities.

Special educators: Special educators support students in inclusive classrooms. This book identifies approaches, strategies, and suggestions for supporting all students in inclusive classrooms. Special educators also often oversee the work of paraprofessionals. This book can be used for paraprofessionals and special educators to read and discuss together in an in-service or book club format.

General educators: General educators are an important part of the classroom team. Learning more about paraprofessionals and support strategies allows general educators to offer a seamless and thoughtful integration of services.

Administrators: This book is an invaluable resource for principals who oversee paraprofessionals and seek to build schoolwide inclusive practices.

Parents of students with special needs: Parents can benefit from this book by understanding the best practices for paraprofessional support in inclusive classrooms. For them, this book can be a resource to secure the appropriate training and support for the paraprofessional working with their child.

Professional development personnel: This book offers new approaches for supporting students with disabilities. Paraprofessionals are the least trained individuals who nonetheless support the most challenging students in our schools. They need training, support, and resources. This book is a useful supplement to any paraprofessional training.

Acknowledgments

This book is about support—meaningful, thoughtful, humanistic support—that allows people to reach their full potential, become their best selves, and do their best work. Support is not only for those we deem in need of support; it is a human need that is essential for everyone. Support isn't just for those we think of as "different" or "special." This work is a call for a different paradigm in schools—where support is available for all to create a community essential for learning.

Indeed, this book and my own academic career would not have been possible without all sorts of support that give me the "feeling of confidence"—in schools and college classrooms, on academic panels, and in school district in-services. Therefore, I feel it is necessary to thank the sizeable community of students, teachers, scholars, family, and friends who have supported me in both visible and invisible ways as I have written this book. This journey is driven by a vision of substantive and meaningful inclusion for all children. I want to thank the many individuals who have helped me see the importance of the journey, imagine the route, and stay the course.

To my students: I have worked with many students over the years, and each taught me something new. I would especially like to thank those who have forced me to think in new ways: Chelsea, Joryann, Ricki, Josh, Moua, Brett, Shawnee, Adam, Trevor, and Gabe.

To the paraprofessionals: I have worked with excellent paraprofessionals and would like to specifically thank Jill Murray and Julie Olstadt, who were great teachers on the topic of being a paraprofessional. I also wish to thank the countless paraprofessionals who have welcomed me into their classrooms, allowed me to follow them around, and willingly provided interviews. Thank you, Sue Gilberti and Kathy Hartman, who read this book and provided me with excellent feedback. Throughout my teaching career, Jill and several other paraprofessionals have helped me to grow as a teacher as I learned from them and we learned together from children.

To my teaching partner: Kathie Crandall, my friend, who taught me that laughter is truly the best indicator of learning.

To my teachers: Lou Brown, whose belief in inclusion has inspired me throughout my entire academic career; and Alice Udvari-Solner, who has sustained me with her intellectual vision, creativity, and commitment to *all* children. Your work has touched every aspect of this book, and it is impossible to say where your influence ends. I also thank Kimber Malmgren and Colleen Capper, whose mentorship has made my career in education possible.

As Jamie Burke suggested, navigation through the complicated dance of steps can take you to the feeling of confidence.

To my friends and colleagues: Christy Ashby, Sharon Dotger, Paula Kluth, Michael Giangreco, Doug Biklen, Corrine Roth Smith, Beth Ferri, Kathy Dempf-Aldrich, Ben Dotger, Thomas Bull, Corrie Burdick, Meghan Cosier, Tara Affolter, Steve Hoffman, and Jerry Hoffman. You have helped me through this complicated dance of steps and help me daily to feel confident (and sane) each day.

To Brookes Publishing Co.: I thank Rebecca Lazo and all of the Brookes staff for your helpful suggestions and creative vision.

To my family: I thank Athan Theoharis, Jeanne Theoharis, and Gail Andre for careful and thoughtful editing. Also, thank you to Nancy Theoharis, Liz Theoharis, Jeff Causton, and Kristine Causton for being excited about the importance of my work.

To my husband, George Theoharis: Thank you, George, for always walking along-side me and for your love, visible and invisible support, and tireless commitment to these issues. Your work to make schools better places for all children is a constant source of my inspiration.

I dedicate this work to my children, Ella and Sam.
You have taught me more in 7 years
than I have learned in a lifetime.
Thank you for being a constant reminder
of the importance of this work
and for the sheer and complete joy you bring me.

1

The
Paraprofessional

HAVING BEEN A PARAEDUCATOR FOR A
COUPLE OF YEARS, DOROTHY KNEW THAT
THE FINAL CLAUSE COULD MEAN
JUST ABOUT ANYTHING.

I was told I got the job, and I vaguely knew what that meant. I knew I would be supporting a student named Helena, but before school started, I hadn't met her and I wasn't really sure what I would be doing day in and day out. To me, I thought it might be a good idea to have some information or training about what the job of paraprofessional really entailed.

—Sue (paraprofessional)

Like Sue, paraprofessionals are hired each year with various amounts of training or knowledge about how to support students with disabilities. This book is meant to provide essential knowledge and guidance about 1) what it means to be a paraprofessional, 2) basic information about special education, 3) inclusive education, 4) how to work within a team, 5) new ideas about how to think about the students you support, 6) how to provide social supports, 7) academic supports, 8) behavioral supports, and finally 9) how to take care of yourself while doing this important work. Let's start by walking together into a kindergarten classroom and meeting a student named Helena.

∙∙∙∙∙∙∙∙∙∙

Helena arrives in her kindergarten classroom. Helena's friend Sam greets her. Both students talk excitedly for a little bit about their weekend as they proceed to the folder bucket. A paraprofessional helps Helena remove her take-home folder and puts it into the rectangular bucket. A paraprofessional then helps Helena remove her jacket, boots, and mittens. Sam races ahead to his table, and Helena drives her wheelchair to her table. The paraprofessional follows.

Helena is a creative, bright little girl who is supported by a paraprofessional. Because she has cerebral palsy, she needs someone to assist her with several tasks throughout her school day. The paraprofessional assigned to her positions her on the floor for circle time, helps her use her computer to answer questions in class, writes down her ideas for stories and assignments, and facilitates social interactions with the other children in her class. Because of the nature of her physical disability, Helena needs regular and ongoing adult support.

∙∙∙∙∙∙∙∙∙∙

This chapter will familiarize you with the job of paraprofessional. I will outline the history of paraprofessionals, a definition of *paraprofessional*, the roles of paraprofessionals, the benefits of paraprofessionals, the different types of settings for paraprofessionals, the most common tasks for paraprofessionals, and some commonly asked questions.

Many professions have job responsibilities that mirror the roles of paraprofessionals. In restaurants, sous-chefs help to prepare dishes by cutting and chopping food for chefs to put together in their final masterpieces. In medicine, physician assistants support doctors in providing medical care to patients. In law, paralegals perform essential tasks, such as filing briefs and drafting documents, to support the work of lawyers. In education, paraprofessionals support the work of teachers in educating students.

In classrooms, paraprofessionals are analogous to each of these professions in certain ways, working under the direction of qualified teachers and special educators. Although the role of paraprofessionals is not to plan or design classroom instruction, they can make important contributions to classroom instruction when they effectively implement important delegated tasks for which they are specifically trained. Paraprofessionals can be very useful supports that help keep classrooms running efficiently and effectively (Causton-Theoharis, Giangreco, Doyle, & Vadasy, 2007).

THE HISTORY OF PARAPROFESSIONALS

The responsibilities of paraprofessionals have changed over time. The history of inclusive education has had a large impact on the employment of paraprofessionals (Giangreco & Doyle, 2002). It has only been since the passage of the Education for All Handicapped Children Act of 1975 (PL 94-142) that students with disabilities have had a legally protected right to attend public school. Before this time, students with disabilities were educated mainly in the home, in segregated settings, or in institutions. As a result, before 1975, paraprofessionals mainly worked in these separate settings for only children with disabilities. It was believed that students with disabilities could not learn as much as students without disabilities and that they did not need certified teachers to support them; therefore, students with disabilities were typically supported by people in paraprofessional roles (Brown, Farrington, Knight, Ross, & Ziegler, 1999).

In the 1970s and 1980s, however, a strong, parent-driven push was started to educate children with disabilities in general education settings alongside students without disabilities. At this time, the regular education initiative began (Will, 1986), and parents began to learn about the idea of *mainstreaming* or *inclusion*. The role of paraprofessionals accordingly shifted as students with disabilities began participating in general education classrooms. At this time, paraprofessionals began to provide greater academic support.

By the 1990s, a wider array of students with more significant disabilities was included in classrooms across all grade levels in school, and there was a large boom in the hiring of paraprofessionals. From 2000 to the present, inclusive education has been more of a legal mandate, particularly with the reauthorization of the Individuals with Disabilities Education Improvement Act (IDEA) of 2004 (PL 108-446). Therefore, the use of paraprofessionals to support students in inclusive settings has increased steadily (U.S. Department of Education, 2007). Now, because students with many more significant disabilities are being included in general education settings, paraprofessionals are more critical than ever.

WHAT DOES PARAPROFESSIONAL MEAN?

The job title *paraprofessional* is described in section 14B of IDEA 2004:

> Paraprofessionals... who are appropriately trained and supervised, in accordance with State law, regulations, or written policy... are to be used to assist in the provision of special education and related services... to children with disabilities. (20 U.S.C. § 1412)

In other words, paraprofessionals are hired to support special education services for children with disabilities. You should be trained and supervised by trained general and special educators; your training should begin before you start to work in the schools, and it should continue throughout your career.

The No Child Left Behind Act (NCLB) of 2001 (PL 107-110) defines *paraprofessional* as someone who "is employed in a preschool, elementary school, or secondary school under the supervision of a certified or licensed teacher, including individuals employed in language instruction, educational programs, special education, or migrant education" (20 U.S.C. § 119).

The qualifications for paraprofessionals have changed since 2001. According to NCLB, all paraprofessionals should have

A. completed at least 2 years of study at an institution of higher education

B. obtained an associate (or higher) degree

C. met a rigorous standard of quality and can demonstrate through a formal academic assessment
    a. knowledge of, and the ability to assist in instruction, reading, writing, and mathematics; or
    b. knowledge of, and the ability to assist in instructing reading readiness, writing readiness, and mathematics readiness, as appropriate. (20 U.S.C. § 6319 [c])

I have listed the legal definition of *paraprofessional* and the legal qualifications for doing the job; now, let's discuss what this means in practical terms and what you actually will be doing.

PARAPROFESSIONAL: FROM CAREGIVER TO LEARNING FACILITATOR

The role of paraprofessionals is essential in public schools today. Paraprofessionals in the United States number more than a half million, and that number is increasing (U.S. Department of Education, 2007). This increase is attributable to many factors. The number has increased primarily because many more students with more significant disabilities (e.g., autism spectrum disorders and cognitive disabilities) are included in general education classrooms. In addition, there has been a slow increase in the number of students who are being identified as having disabilities. Many educators view the support of a paraprofessional as key for an inclusive classroom. In other words, students are included in general education settings because they are accompanied by paraprofessionals.

Moreover, the role of paraprofessionals has become much more complex as it has moved from caregiver to facilitator. In the past, students with disabilities were warehoused in rooms for only children with disabilities, and the supports they received were more related to personal care and keeping them occupied. Educational goals for students with significant disabilities were essentially limited to life skills and job-related tasks. For example, common activities for such students, regardless of age, were to place pegs into peg boards, practice dressing, or use appropriate table manners. As a result, the role of paraprofessionals was mainly caregiving. Now, educators in the field have learned that students with disabilities are just as capable of learning as their general education counterparts. Consequently, the goals many students now have in their individualized education programs (IEPs) closely resemble those of their same-age peers. Paraprofessionals are now responsible for helping to educate students using materials appropriate to their grade levels and for helping to facilitate complex social networks and friendships. Because of these new roles, paraprofessionals have become integral members of teaching teams with increasingly challenging new responsibilities.

MY TITLE IS TEACHING ASSISTANT. IS THAT THE SAME THING?

You might not be called a *paraprofessional;* instead, you might be called a *teaching assistant* or another term. Just as the job has evolved, the title *paraprofessional* has changed over time and still varies from district to district. The terms *aide, assistant, one-to-one, teacher aide, program assistant, clerical assistant,* and *teaching assistant* commonly are used to describe the role of paraprofessionals. Although this title varies, many times the job responsibilities are similar but distinguishable by the number of students that the person supports. A one-to-one assistant tends to support a single student, a teaching assistant usually supports more students, a clerical assistant tends to do more work with the materials for instruction, and a program assistant typically supports an entire classroom.

THE ROLE OF PARAPROFESSIONALS TODAY

Paraprofessionals have varied responsibilities. Your role is likely determined by the unique needs of the students you support and the unique classroom context. These responsibilities typically include supporting children socially, academically, physically, and behaviorally. Social support includes helping children make and maintain friendships with other children. For example, a paraprofessional might assist a student in communicating with a peer, in selecting a partner for group work, or in finding a friend to play with at recess time.

Academic support involves helping students as they attend to academic content and learn new material. For example, you might be responsible for helping a student prepare for a test, outline a chapter, or put together an insect collection. Any academic task that students do in school may require paraprofessional support.

Some children also require physical support. For example, a child using a wheelchair may need help when eating, dressing, or transferring from a seated to a standing position. Because of the nature of their physical disability, some students require more physical support than others.

Another common responsibility involves providing behavioral supports. An example of this type of support is giving a child something to do with her or his hands so that the student can pay attention during a read-aloud story or lecture. Or, you may provide positive reinforcement at key times or help a student take movement breaks throughout the day so that he or she is better able to stay on task during seated instructional time.

The student's IEP will be a framework for the amount and type of support you provide. The team of teachers you work with should help you identify your roles within the classroom. Generally speaking, your role will be to reinforce and reteach skills; help support behavior control; and, possibly, provide personal care or mobility support. Because each student is unique, your job will differ according to the needs of the students you will be supporting.

BENEFITS OF PARAPROFESSIONALS

Paraprofessionals offer crucial support that is helpful to both teachers and students. When well trained, they expand learning opportunities by giving students repeated practice with skills or experiences. They provide students more individualized instruction. The presence of a paraprofessional allows teachers to have more planning time. Students with disabilities can be more carefully monitored, supported, and generally involved in instruction to a greater extent.

IN WHAT SETTINGS MIGHT I WORK?

Inclusive Classrooms

Although this book focuses on supporting students in inclusive classrooms, you might find yourself in different types of classrooms. Inclusive classrooms are generally places in which students with and without disabilities are educated together. Other terms you might hear are *general education classroom*, *third-grade classroom*, or *typical classroom*. A more outdated term for an inclusive classroom is a *mainstreamed classroom*. More information about inclusion can be found in Chapter 3.

Resource Rooms

A resource room is a place in which students are generally supposed to spend a short amount of time working on a specific skill or subject before returning to the general education classroom. The instruction in these classrooms is typically delivered in a small group with one teacher teaching a small group of students or with one teacher working directly with one student.

Self-Contained Classrooms

A self-contained classroom is designed for the instruction of only students who have disabilities. The purpose of this kind of classroom was initially to group students who had similar learning needs. These kinds of classrooms are very controversial because students in self-contained classrooms interact on a very limited basis, if at all, with students who do not have disabilities.

Community-Based Classrooms

Some paraprofessionals work in community-based classrooms. The idea behind community-based instruction is that some students require instruction to prepare them for life in the community by working on job skills and independent living skills. Therefore, some students receive their instruction in the community. Some types of community-based locations include job sites, recreational facilities, grocery stores, or other community locations.

WHAT DOES A PARAPROFESSIONAL DO?

Although you should not be expected to do windows, as the cartoon on the opening page jokingly suggests, paraprofessionals engage in many different daily responsibilities. Those job tasks vary from school to school. Generally, if you work in a school, the types of responsibilities you can expect to do fall under the categories of *instructional tasks, behavioral support tasks, clerical tasks, supervision tasks, planning or preparation,* and *personal care tasks* (Giangreco, Broer, & Edelman, 2002). Table 1.1 describes each type of task and provides an example. To be clear, these are types of tasks that you could be assigned, but you may be assigned to other tasks as well.

Job tasks also depend on the type of support you are assigned to give. If you work in a resource room, you will likely provide one-to-one instruction and small-group instruction. You might be responsible for student observation and data collection with regard to academic support or behavioral support. You also might supervise students on the playground, at lunch, or on the bus, helping to support student behavior control, or you might take on more clerical tasks to support teaching and learning, such as typing, recording grades, and photocopying (French, 1998).

Table 1.1. Typical responsibilities of paraprofessionals

Type of task	Examples of tasks
Instructional tasks	Reviewing vocabulary with a student
	Reteaching a math method
	Prereading a book with a student
	Running a center at center time
Behavioral support tasks	Providing positive reinforcement
	Addressing sensory needs
	Following a behavior plan
	Helping a student calm down
Clerical tasks	Making copies
	Creating modifications
	Enlarging materials (increasing font size)
Supervision tasks	Supervising students on the playground, on the bus, or in the cafeteria
Planning or preparation tasks	Making a game
	Creating a communication board
	Preparing or labeling materials
Personal care tasks	Helping students dress after physical education
	Providing support while students put on or take off outdoor clothing
	Assisting students in brushing hair or teeth
	Helping students use the restroom

COMMONLY ASKED QUESTIONS ABOUT THE ROLE OF PARAPROFESSIONALS

Q. To whom do I report?

A. Typically, a paraprofessional reports to the special education teacher to whom he or she is assigned. After that, a building principal or director of special education would be next in the chain of command. However, you will also work closely with general education teachers and related services providers (e.g., occupational therapists, physical therapists, speech and language teachers), and they may provide guidance as well.

Q. How can I obtain a copy of my job description?

A. You can typically request a copy of your job description by talking to someone in human resources or by asking the director of special education. Most districts will provide you a written job description if you do not already have one.

Q. Can I lead a small-group discussion?

A. Yes, you can lead a small-group discussion or review material with students under the direction of a certified teacher. You are not allowed to introduce new material, but you can reinforce material taught previously by a certified teacher.

Q. Can I teach an entire class by myself?

A. A paraprofessional generally does not teach an entire class new material, but he or she could be responsible for reading a book aloud to the class or supporting the work of the entire class, under the direction and supervision of a certified teacher.

Q. Who is ultimately responsible for the education of the student I am supporting?

A. The special education teacher and general education teacher assigned to the student are responsible. The terms *case manager* or *service coordinator* are sometimes used to refer to the special education teacher assigned to the student.

Q. Should I work from written plans? .

A. Yes, you should work from written plans If you don't have written plans, you can request them from the special education teacher working with you. It is important to note that the plans that are provided will not account for every minute of the day; instead, typically they will consist of a schedule and tasks for periods of the day.

CONCLUSION

Understanding your roles and responsibilities is essential for you to do your job effectively. This chapter has surveyed the history of paraprofessionals, discussed the roles and responsibilities of paraprofessionals today, and provided answers to some commonly asked questions. As you can see, paraprofessionals support students who receive special education services. Therefore, the next chapter is designed to give you some background about special education.

NOTES

✺ 2 ✺

Special Education

WHAT DO YOU CHOOSE TO SEE?
WEEDS OR WILDFLOWERS?

My first week on the job, I was completely overwhelmed. After that week, I went to a work party with my husband. During the party one of my husband's coworkers asked me what I do for a living. I told her that I was a special education assistant. She asked me what I meant by "special education." I stopped . . . . I had to laugh . . . at that moment I realized . . . I had no idea what to say.

—Tonya (paraprofessional)

I begin with the question that many have asked when they began work in this field. What is special education? In this chapter, I answer that question along with the following ones: Who receives special education? What does *disability* mean? Why should people be cautious of labels? What does all this terminology mean? What are the different categories of disabilities? At the end of this chapter, I also answer other commonly asked questions.

This chapter identifies the important concepts and ideas that are essential for anyone in the field of special education to understand. By knowing this information, paraprofessionals can understand the bigger educational system of which they are now part.

WHAT IS SPECIAL EDUCATION?

Simply put, *special education* is individualized instruction designed to meet the unique needs of certain students. This type of customized instruction may require a student to have accommodations or modifications to his or her class work. *Accommodations* are adaptations to the curriculum that do not fundamentally alter or lower standards (e.g., test location, student response method). *Modifications* are changes to the curriculum that do alter the expectations. Examples of modifications include changes to the course content, timing, or test presentation. Any student who receives special education services may receive specialized materials (e.g., books on tape), services (e.g., speech and language services), equipment (e.g., a communication system), or different teaching strategies (e.g., visual notes) (Disabilities Education Improvement Act [IDEA] of 2004 [PL 108-446]). For example, a student who is deaf may require the services of a sign language interpreter so that she can follow along in the classroom. A student who has autism may require specialized materials such as a visual schedule to prepare him for the changing routines in his day. A student with a learning disability may require additional reading instruction or extended time for completing her written assignments.

Special education is a part of general education. It is a system of supports to help students learn the general education curriculum. The legal definition under IDEA 2004 of *special education* is "specially designed instruction, at no cost to the child's parents, to meet the needs of a student with a disability" (20 U.S.C. § 1401 [25]).

This definition recognizes that some children have difficulty learning, behaving, or physically accessing general education and, because of such disabilities, need individualized supports to help them to build their skills and abilities to reach their full potential in school. These additional services do not cost the students' parents any money and are funded by the local and federal governments.

SPECIAL EDUCATION IS A SERVICE, NOT A PLACE

In the past, when the term *special education* was used, a special place came to mind. People thought of a room, a school, or other separate places to which children with disabilities went to receive different and special education. This notion, however, is rapidly changing. Special education is now not limited to a specific location. It has been established that all children—even children with autism, severe disabilities, and emotional or behavioral disabilities—learn best in classroom settings with their general education peers (Causton-Theoharis & Theoharis, 2008; Peterson & Hittie, 2002). Special education services are portable services (e.g., help with reading, math, or speech skills) that can be brought directly to individual children. Special education occurs in general education classrooms all over the United States and the rest of the world. When students with disabilities are educated primarily in general education settings, this is called *inclusive education.* In inclusive classrooms, teachers and para professionals should ensure that children with special needs are part of the general education curriculum, instruction, and social scene as much as possible within the least restrictive environment. The next chapter on inclusive education will describe more fully the concept of *least restrictive environment.*

WHO RECEIVES SPECIAL EDUCATION?

Every year, under IDEA 2004, more than 6 million students in the United States between the ages of 3 and 21 receive special education services (U.S. Department of Education, 2007). In other words, roughly 11% of all school-age children qualify for special education services because they have disabilities.

Under IDEA 2004, the definition of a student with a disability is "one who has certain disabilities and who, because of the impairment, needs special education and related services" (20 U.S.C. § 1401 [3]). Each student qualifies for special education because he or she has one or more type of disability. Each of the different types of disabilities is defined and described later in this chapter.

When one examines the population of students who receive special education, several disturbing trends appear in the areas of gender, socioeconomic status, and race. First, even though the numbers of males and females in the general school population are equal, the population receiving special education is roughly two-thirds male (U.S. Department of Education, 2007). Second, the poverty rate is proportionately much higher among students who qualify for special education than in the entire school population (U.S. Department of Education, 2007). Lastly, a disproportionate number of certain racial or ethnic groups are served in special education. For example, because African Americans make up 14% of the general population, one might assume that only 14% of students who qualify for special education would be African American (Turnbull, Turnbull, Shank, & Smith, 2004). In fact, African American students represent 44.9% of the total number of students labeled as having learning disabilities (U.S. Department of Education, 2007). Further, African American students are three times more likely than Caucasian students to receive special education and related services.

WHAT DOES DISABILITY MEAN?

Disability categories are used to "classify and think about the problems developing children may encounter" (Contract Consultants, IAC, 1997, p. 8, as cited in Kluth, 2003). Understanding a student's label is only the beginning point in learning about a child. A child's disability label reveals nothing about the student's individual gifts, talents, and strengths. A disability is one of many parts of a student. A disability does not describe who a person is; it describes only one aspect of the person.

To illustrate this point, take a moment to write down five descriptors about yourself. What did you include? For me, I might include descriptors about who I am in relation to others, or my profession, or personality traits. My list might include *mother, professor, lover of nature, daughter,* and *outgoing.* Interestingly, my list did not include my deficiencies. I do not think of myself generally as someone who cannot read maps or who does not balance her checkbook very well. The same is true for any individual with a disability. That person's area of disability is one (possibly very small) part of who he or she is.

SOCIAL CONSTRUCTION OF DISABILITY

It is also important to recognize that people create disability categories and that those categories shift and change over time. Medical professionals, teachers, and researchers, along with the federal government, have created these categories. These are not static categories; they do and have changed. An extreme example of how disability is constructed is that, at one point in time, to qualify for having a cognitive disability (or mental retardation, as used in federal legislation), a person needed to have an IQ of 80 or below. In 1973, the federal government lowered the cutoff IQ score to 70 points or below. So, in essence, with the single swish of a pen, hundreds of thousands of people were "cured" of mental retardation (Ashby, 2008; Blatt, 1987).

Once created, these categories are reinforced. In other words, people see mainly what they are looking for. Once a student is assigned a label, educators begin seeing the child through a different lens—the lens of disability. As I was observing a student for a research project in a third-grade classroom, I observed this very notion. All of the students were busy working and talking as they finished their art projects. The room was bustling and busy. Suddenly, the art teacher shouted, "Jamie, that is the last time." The teacher walked to the chalkboard and wrote Jamie's name down. Nearly all of the students were talking, yet Jamie, who happens to have a label of *emotional disturbance,* was noticed for being too talkative or out of line. From where I was sitting, Jamie's behavior looked no different than that of many of the other students.

Disability categories are created, and then people determine who qualifies and who does not. Have you ever worked with someone who had a label even though you really did not think he or she had a disability? Have you ever seen a student who did not qualify for special education even though you thought he or she might? Disability labels are not hard and fast rules that describe people; they are indicators of patterns of difficulty for individuals and are determined by the perceptions of other people.

LABELS: PROCEED WITH CAUTION

On the one hand, many believe labels to be helpful for defining a common language for parents and professionals. This common language allows students access to certain supports and services that they need. In a way, a label is the necessary first step toward certain services (including the services of a paraprofessional).

On the other hand, there are real problems with the labeling or categorizing of individuals. Kliewer and Biklen (1996) state that labeling students can be a "demeaning process frequently contributing to stigmatization and leading to social and educational isolation" (p. 83). The use of and overreliance on disability labels poses many problems. Disability labels can lead to stereotyping by causing teachers to see certain students in one, and only one, way. Labeling tends to highlight the differences among people. For example, when a student is assigned a label, teachers and paraprofessionals begin to notice the differences between that student and his or her peers. Labels can lead to poor self-esteem as students begin to see themselves differently because of such labels. Lastly, labels convey the impression of permanence, even though, in some cases, students are only "disabled" when they are in school. Unfortunately, labels give professionals a real sense of security. They allow professionals to believe that "disability categories are static, meaningful, and well understood when in fact they are none of these things" (Kluth, 2003, p. 7).

Throughout this book, I use the language that is most common to the current educational system. I am well aware, however, of the real problems and, at times, dangers of thinking about difference in these ways. Some people use the term *dis/ability* (with a slash) to indicate that all students should focus on their individual abilities. Although I prefer the word *dis/ability,* I am purposefully using the language most common to education so that my readers can easily connect this information to other information from the field.

WHAT ARE THEY SAYING? EDUCATIONAL TERMINOLOGY

Alphabet soup: that is how I sometimes describe the use of acronyms in the field of special education. Understanding the language of special education can take a long time. The following is an alphabetical listing of several educational terms that are often used as acronyms:

- ADD/ADHD: attention deficit disorder and/or attention-deficit/hyperactivity disorder
- BIP: behavior intervention plan
- CBI: community-based instruction
- DS: Down syndrome
- EBD: emotional behavioral disturbance
- ED: emotional disturbance
- ESY: extended school year
- FAPE: free appropriate public education
- FBA: functional behavioral assessment
- HI: hearing impaired
- IDEA: Individuals with Disabilities Education Act
- IEP: individualized education program
- LRE: least restrictive environment
- MR: mental retardation
- OI: orthopedic impairment
- OT: occupational therapist
- PBS: positive behavioral support
- PT: physical therapist
- SL: speech and language
- SLD: specific learning disability
- SLP: speech-language pathologist
- TBI: traumatic brain injury
- VI: visual impairment

FEDERALLY RECOGNIZED CATEGORIES OF DISABILITY

How many different categories of disabilities are you aware of? There are 13 federal categories of disability. Every student who receives special education services has received a formal label representing 1 of the 13 categories. Now, without looking ahead, take a moment to jot down on a separate piece of paper as many of the 13 disability categories as you can. Compare your list with the information provided in the next paragraph.

The 13 categories of disability include the following: 1) autism, 2) deafblindness, 3) deafness, 4) emotional disturbance, 5) hearing impairment, 6) mental retardation, 7) multiple disabilities, 8) orthopedic impairments, 9) other health impairments, 10) specific learning disabilities, 11) speech and language impairments, 12) traumatic brain injury, and 13) visual impairment including blindness. I have included the IDEA 2004 definition for each; however, the most useful way to understand each disability is to listen carefully to the people who have been labeled with the disability and understand the disability deeply. Therefore, after each of the definitions, I include the voices of people who have been labeled with each of the particular disabilities. These voices are not meant to be examples; one person cannot possibly represent the entire population of students who have the same disability. Note the differences between the legal definitions and the definitions that the people themselves use. It is interesting that the legal definitions focus on what students cannot do or the difficulties that they have, whereas the other voices focus more on the gifts and abilities of each individual.

Autism

Autism is defined by law as a developmental disability that significantly affects verbal and nonverbal communication and social interaction and adversely affects educational performance; autism is generally evident before age 3. Characteristics often associated with autism are engaging in repetitive activities and stereotyped movements, resistance to change in daily routines or the environment, and unusual responses to sensory experiences (34 C.F.R. § 300.8 [c][1][i]).

Two people who have autism and live with it every day offer a quite different definition of the disability:

> Some aspects of autism may be good or bad depending only on how they are perceived.
>
> For example, hyperfocusing is a problem if you're hyperfocusing on your feet and miss the traffic light change. On the other hand, hyperfocusing is a great skill for working on intensive projects. This trait is particularly well suited to freelancers and computer work. I would never argue that autism is all good or merely a difference. I do find that my autism is disabling. However, that doesn't mean that it is all bad or that I mean I want to be someone else. (Molton 2000)

Another individual with autism describes it this way: "I believe Autism is a marvelous occurrence of nature, not a tragic example of the human mind gone wrong. In many cases, Autism can also be a kind of genius undiscovered" (O'Neill, 1999, p. 14, as cited in Kluth, 2003, p. 3).

Deafblindness

Deafblindness is defined by law as concomitant [simultaneous] hearing and visual impairments, the combination of which causes such severe communication and other developmental and educational needs that they cannot be accommodated in special education programs solely for children with deafness or children with blindness (34 C.F.R. § 300.8 [c][2]).

In other words, students with deafblindness have both hearing and visual impairments. The population of students with deafblindness constitutes only 0.0001% of the special education population. Therefore, you probably will not support someone with this disability label. Many people who are deaf and blind learn to use tactile sign, a form of sign language that is felt with the hands.

Helen Keller is one of the most famous examples of a person with deafblindness. She wrote very articulately about what it was like to live with this label in her autobiography entitled *The Story of My Life.* One quote from Helen Keller (1903) describes how she accessed the world: "The best and most beautiful things in the world cannot be seen or even touched. They must be felt within the heart."

Deafness

Deafness is legally defined as a hearing impairment so severe that a child's educational performance is adversely affected; people with deafness have difficulty, with or without amplification, in processing linguistic information (34 C.F.R. § 300.8 [c][3]). Students who qualify for special education under the category of deafness typically use sign language. These individuals can access the general education curriculum through the use of a sign language interpreter, through oral methods of speech reading, or by reading other people's lips and facial expressions.

A deaf man identified as Mavis shares his experiences living as a deaf person:

> It is true. Every weekend, I ride my high quality road racing bicycle at high speeds (sometime as fast as 40 mph on the flats) with a bunch of men from my bicycle club. I am the only deaf person in that 500 member club. I also enjoy going to the shooting range to fire handguns and socialize. (Mavis, 2003, p. 3)

Emotional Disturbance

Emotional disturbance is legally defined as a condition exhibiting one or more of the following characteristics for a long period of time and to a marked degree that adversely affects a child's educational performance:

a. An inability to learn that cannot be explained by intellectual, sensory, or health factors.

b. An inability to build or maintain satisfactory interpersonal relationships with peers and teachers.

c. Inappropriate types of behavior or feelings under normal circumstances.

d. A general pervasive mood of unhappiness or depression.

e. A tendency to develop physical symptoms or fears associated with personal or school problems. (34 C.F.R. § 300.8 [c][4][i])

These students make up 8% of the special education population. This category of disability relates to how students behave. For a student to qualify for this category of disability, the student's behavior should look significantly different than that of his or her peers (Taylor, Smiley, & Richards, 2009).

Kerri, who has emotional disturbance, describes it this way:

> I misinterpret half of what [people] say to me and translate it to mean they don't want to be my friend anymore. Why should they? I am not worth their time or love or attention. Then I get angry with them and I turn on them. Hurt them before they can hurt me. It is so stupid, and I realize it later, but only after it is too late. (OrganizedWisdom, 2008, p. 16)

Hearing Impairment

Being identified as having a *hearing impairment* means that there is an impairment in hearing, whether permanent or fluctuating, that adversely affects a child's educational performance but that is not included under the definition of *deafness* (34 C.F.R. § 300.8 [c][5]). Students who have hearing impairments generally do not use sign language, because the hearing that they do have is useful to them. Instead, they might use an amplification system and receive training on lipreading.

One individual (Sarahjane Thompson) with hearing impairment describes her experience:

> The way I tend to explain [hearing impairment] is that it's not necessarily that you can't hear the words that people are using, it's that you hear sounds that resemble words, but you can't quite figure out what the sounds are. Like when a hearing person only just hears something, and asks someone to repeat themselves. Like that. Except for me it's way more frequent. So that's why I tend to use other strategies to figure out what's going on. I lip-read . . . . But lip-reading isn't perfect. A lot of the words look the same and so it's hard for me to use it exclusively to talk to someone. I tend to guess a lot. I'll catch most of a sentence and then sort of try to fill in the gaps myself. Usually it works. Sometimes it doesn't . . . . Every now and then I'll mis-hear an entire sentence and my brain will fill in the random words that sort of fit the syllables and sounds, but together those words do not make sense at all . . . . It's just so normal for me to be hearing impaired. People ask me what it's like to be [hearing impaired] and I just don't have a perfect answer for them. "What's it like to be able to hear?" There's no real comparison and so I don't really know what is different about it. Obviously hearing people can hear more and understand more sounds, but what does that mean? It can be really hard to explain. It's all about perception. (Williams, 2008, p. 13)

Mental Retardation

The *mental retardation* label is legally assigned to students who have significantly sub-average general intellectual functioning, existing concurrently with impairments in adaptive behavior and manifested during the developmental period, that adversely affects a child's educational performance (34 C.F.R. § 300.8 [c][6]). Although the term *mental retardation* is cited in the law, the terms *cognitive disabilities* and *intellectual disabilities* are generally preferred. This category constitutes 11% of the special education population. People with mental retardation vary greatly. Some students have speech and can write, whereas other students do not use speech and are unable to write. Lacking the ability to write or speak, however, does not mean that the person has no ideas or no desire to communicate with others. These students tend to deeply desire connections with others and, when given the tools to communicate, engage with other students and with the content.

What follows is a first-person account from someone labeled with cognitive disabilities:

> What I would like is for you to understand that my biggest problem is not a neurological dysfunction. It is being misunderstood by people who think my problems are due to poor parenting. My mom has really tried to teach me proper social behaviors, but it just does not click all the time. Sometimes I can't remember the social rules. (FAS Community Resource Center, 2008)

This extract from Schalock and Braddock (2002) places among broader context Ollie Webb's words about her life with mental retardation:

> I was often the target of cruel jokes. It was easy to take advantage of me. People called me retarded . . . I worked out there—17 years—and I made salads, sandwiches, and soup, and washed pots and pans. You name it, I done it out there . . . . One time I came in and the boss said, "I am going to take you off of salads." I said, "Why?" He said, "Cause you can't read." I said, "It make no difference. I can make salads and sandwiches." I said, "It make no damn difference." . . . It came time to leave the sad word *retarded* [to history] . . . . To say that people should be known by their names [and accomplishments], not by their disabilities, I ain't different from you. I am the same as you. I got a name, and I want you to call me by my name. My name is Ollie ... Webb. (pp. 55–57)

Multiple Disabilities

The term *multiple disabilities* is legally defined as concomitant impairments (e.g., mental retardation–blindness, mental retardation–orthopedic impairment), the combination of which causes such severe educational needs that they cannot be accommodated in a special educational setting solely for one of the impairments. The term does not include deafblindness (34 C.F.R. § 300.8 [c][7]).

Roughly 2% of the special education population are considered to have multiple disabilities. Therefore, it is unlikely that you will work with someone who has that label.

Orthopedic Impairments

The term *orthopedic impairment* means a severe orthopedic impairment that adversely affects a child's educational performance. The term includes impairments caused by congenital impairments (e.g., clubfoot, absence of a body part), impairments caused by disease (e.g., poliomyelitis, bone tuberculosis), and impairments from other causes (e.g., cerebral palsy, amputations, fractures or burns that cause contractures) (34 C.F.R. § 300.8 [c][8]).

Angela Gabel, a high school student with cerebral palsy who uses a wheelchair, describes herself and her experience in school as follows:

> When you see me, I think the first thing you would notice is that I'm a pretty positive person. I love to listen to music, go horseback riding, and draw . . . . When I was in elementary school . . . I had friends and liked to play the same games as everyone else, but the teachers were always worried that I was too fragile and would hurt myself. (Gabel, 2006, p. 35)

Other Health Impairments

Other health impairment is legally defined as having limited strength, vitality, or alertness to environmental stimuli, resulting in limited alertness with respect to the educational environment, that

a. is due to chronic or acute health problems such as asthma, attention deficit disorder or attention deficit hyperactivity disorder, diabetes, epilepsy, a heart condition, hemophilia, lead poisoning, leukemia, nephritis, rheumatic fever, and sickle cell anemia; and

b. adversely affects a child's educational performance. (34 C.F.R. § 300.8 [c][9])

This impairment includes students who have attention-deficit/hyperactivity disorder (ADHD). The label *ADHD* is assigned to students who have difficulty maintaining attention, knowing when to slow down, or organizing themselves to finish tasks (American Psychiatric Association, 2000). Obviously, not everyone who has each of these disorders qualifies for special education, but if such a condition has been diagnosed by a medical professional and adversely affects a student's educational performance (and if the student needs additional supports), he or she is likely to qualify.

Brian explains his life with attention disorders:

> as you can tell by my writing style i run all over the place. give mwe [*sic*] a task and directions it's done asap. give me time to think about it, it's done in my head but i can't complete the task. (*Living with ADD,* 2004)

Specific Learning Disabilities

A *specific learning disability* is legally defined as a disorder in one or more of the basic psychological processes involved in understanding or using spoken or written language; it may manifest itself in an imperfect ability to listen, think, speak, read, write, spell, or do mathematical calculations. The term includes such conditions as perceptual disabilities, brain injury, minimal brain dysfunction, dyslexia, and developmental aphasia. The term does not include learning problems that are primarily the results of visual, hearing, or motor disabilities; of mental retardation; of emotional disturbance; or of environmental, cultural, or economic disadvantages (34 C.F.R. § 300.8 [c][10]).

Almost half of all students categorized as having disabilities fall under this category. This is the most frequently occurring disability; thus, you are quite likely to work with students who have the label of *specific learning disability.*

In an article about being a student with a learning disability, Caitlin Norah Callahan writes about her advice to others:

> I believe one key idea is to find one's own definition of the dual identity within one-self as a learner and as a student. The learner is the one who makes an effort to be curious, involved and motivated. Not all knowledge is taught in school. It is the student identity that gets labeled as the disabled. The "learning disability" should not be allowed to overwhelm one's desire to attain knowledge. The learner in you must prevent it. (Callahan, 1997)

Speech and Language

Speech or language impairment is legally defined as a communication disorder such as stuttering, impaired articulation, a language impairment, or a voice impairment that adversely affects a child's educational performance (34 C.F.R. § 300.8 [c][11]).

This is the second-most-common disability category. Approximately 20% of students who qualify for special education are served under this category. Students who qualify for this disability have a wide range of impairment. Some students who receive speech and language services have difficulty with articulation or fluency (e.g., stuttering). Other students might not use speech. A student who only has speech and language disabilities is not likely to be supported by a paraprofessional. However, many students have speech and language impairments and another disability label that necessitates the support of a paraprofessional.

What follows is a story from a person who did not have speech in his early years but who later was able to communicate through the use of a communication system. This story illustrates the frustration inherent in not having a reliable method of speech:

> I know what it is like to be fed potatoes all my life. After all potatoes are a good basic food for everyday, easy to fix in many different ways. I hate potatoes! But then who knew that but me? I know what it is like to be dressed in reds and blues when my favorite colors are mint greens, lemon yellows, and pinks. I mean really can you imagine [what it is like not to communicate]? Mama found me one night curled up in a ball in my bed crying, doubled over in pain. I couldn't explain to her where or how I hurt. So, after checking me over the best she could, she thought I had a bad stomachache due to constipation. Naturally, a quick cure for that was an enema. It did not help my earache at all! (Paul-Brown & Diggs, 1993, p. 8).

Traumatic Brain Injury

Traumatic brain injury is legally defined as an acquired injury to the brain caused by an external physical force, resulting in total or partial functional disability or psychosocial impairment, or both, that adversely affects a child's educational performance. The term applies to open or closed head injuries resulting in impairments in one or more areas, such as cognition; language; memory; attention; reasoning; abstract thinking; judgment; problem solving; sensory, perceptual, and motor abilities; psychosocial behavior; physical functions; information processing; and speech. The term does not include brain injuries that are congenital, degenerative, or induced by birth trauma (34 C.F.R. § 300.8 [c][12]).

This type of disability differs from the others because it is acquired during the person's lifetime (e.g., car accident or blow to the head). People are not born with this condition—instead, they acquire the disability. The emotional adjustment to acquiring a disability is an issue not only for the student but also for parents/guardians and teachers.

A teenager who endured a traumatic brain injury reflects on what she saw as her new life:

> The three-month coma that followed and the years of rehabilitation are only a blur to me. I slowly awoke over the next two years becoming aware of my surroundings as well as myself and my inabilities, one being that I could no longer sing as I was left with a severe speech impediment. (Parker, 2008)

Visual Impairment Including Blindness

A *visual impairment* is legally defined as an impairment in vision that, even with correction, adversely affects a child's educational performance. The term includes both partial sight and blindness (34 C.F.R. § 300.8 [c][13]).

The services received by students under this category of disability differ depending on the severity or type of visual impairment. Some students with visual impairments use magnifiers and larger-print texts; students who have no vision receive mobility training (or training on how to walk around their environment) and instruction in how to read Braille.

How many students qualify for each of the different types of disabilities? The pie graph shown in Figure 2.1 depicts the percentages of students who receive special education services from ages 6 to 21 and the percentages of students who fall under each of the categories of disabilities. As Figure 2.1 indicates, the high-incidence (or most common) disabilities are learning disabilities, speech and language disabilities, mental retardation, and other health impairment. The rest of the categories are considered low incidence (or not as common).

Now that you have read through each of the definitions of disabilities, I will reiterate the importance of knowing these definitions, but keep in mind that this is only a (very small) step in understanding a student. Chapter 4 focuses more on how to think about students in general, with very little focus on individual disabilities.

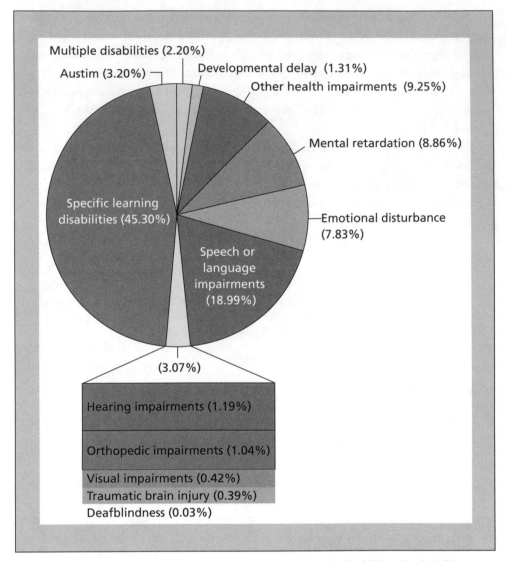

Figure 2.1. Percentage distribution of students (ages 6–21) with disabilities, by disability type, 2005. From Data Accountability Center: Individuals with Disabilities Education Act (IDEA) data. [n.d.]. Retrieved December 1, 2008, from http://www.ideadata.org/docs/PartBTrendData/B2A.html)

COMMONLY ASKED QUESTIONS ABOUT SPECIAL EDUCATION

Q. How can I learn about the students I am supporting?

A. Start by reading each student's individualized education program (IEP). Ask the teacher with whom you are working to show you a copy of the IEP. This document and its contents are confidential and not to be shared with others, but you can have access to a student's IEP. You can also get to know the student by asking questions about his or her likes, dislikes, interests, and struggles.

Here are some questions that would be helpful when getting to know a student:

What do you want me to know about you?

What do you like about school?

What don't you like about school?

What do you enjoy doing outside of school?

Would you tell me about your friends?

How do you prefer to be supported?

What do you need from me?

What don't you want me to do?

You can also ask the teacher about the type of support the student needs. Here are some good questions you could ask:

What is motivating for this student?

What does this student enjoy?

Would you tell me about this student's friends?

How can we support this student's social needs?

What are this student's academic needs?

How can we best support this student's academic needs?

Does this student have challenging behavior?

How can we best support this student's behavior?

Does this student have sensory needs of which I need to be aware?

Does this student have communication needs that I might need to know?

What modifications does this student use?

Does this student use assistive technology?

What else do I need to know about this student?

Q. I do not feel that I am trained to do my job. How can I get some training?

A. You should ask. Start with your building principal or the head of special education in your school. The following elements could be included in an e-mail, phone call, or letter to your supervisors:

- Be specific about the type of training you need. For example, you could say, "In my current position, I need to know more about working with students with autism."

- Ask whether they know of any training that is being offered, or ask whether they could hire someone to come in to work with the school or team.

CONCLUSION

Understanding disability is critical to understanding the larger systems of special education. Nonetheless, the only way to truly understand certain individual students is to get to know people who live with those disabilities. Reading the definitions of the 13 federal categories of disability is just the first step to beginning to understand the students that you support. Having covered some of the basics of special education, I shall commence the joyful work of helping you to learn about individual students and helping to support them in the classroom. The next chapter focuses on including students with disabilities.

NOTES

_____

_____

_____

_____

_____

_____

_____

_____

_____

_____

_____

_____

_____

_____

_____

3

Inclusive Education

THE EVOLUTION OF SWIMMING LESSONS:
SURPRISINGLY SIMILAR TO THE EVOLUTION
OF INCLUDING STUDENTS WITH
DISABILITIES IN GENERAL EDUCATION.

When I think about inclusion, I think about Chelsea. She is a fourth-grade student with Down syndrome. When I went to school, kids like Chelsea did not go to school with me. She rides the bus to her local school with her neighborhood friends, she attends a typical fourth-grade class, she works on reading, writing, math, social studies, science, physical education, lunch, and art alongside her fourth-grade friends. Everything! She is included in all aspects of the school day. To me, this is all new.

—Peter (paraprofessional)

In the not-so-distant past, and in many other school districts, Chelsea would be in a separate class for students who had disabilities. Luckily, today, she is educated in an inclusive setting along with many other students with more significant disabilities. Being part of her classroom and peer group is just part of her daily experience. In this chapter, I identify the concepts necessary to understanding inclusive education such as belonging, the history of inclusive education, major legal concepts, the definition of inclusive education, indicators of inclusive education, individualized education programs (IEPs), and commonly asked questions.

BELONGING

To be rooted is perhaps the most important and least recognized need of the human soul.

—Simone Weil (2001)

One central reason that kids are being included in general education settings is that every child, with or without disabilities, has the right to belong. All human beings desire friendships, relationships, and academic challenge. Kids with disabilities are no different.

Think for a moment about yourself. Think of a time you felt that you truly belonged somewhere. Was it a group, a club, a sports team, or a work environment? Now think about your behavior in that setting. How did you behave? How did you feel? If someone looked at you, how did you act? Most people are more willing to take risks, to contribute, to share, and to learn in such environments. When you feel connected to a group of people, you are likely more talkative, more engaged, and more willing to be yourself. The same is true for children.

Now, on the contrary, think of a time that you felt you did not belong or were ostracized from a group. How did you behave? How did you feel? In those situations, many people respond by being withdrawn and quiet, shutting themselves off from the group. Or, a person might respond by leaving the situation or getting angry. The same is true for children in school. It is essential to feel connected to a group or part of the school community. Not only is this important for self-worth, but it is also important for learning.

Table 3.1. Feelings associated with inclusion and exclusion

When I was included	When I was excluded
I felt loved	I was angry
I felt cared for	I was withdrawn
I took risks	I was quiet
I felt smart	I was hurt
I was myself	I cried
I laughed often	I felt sick
I was creative	I did not participate
I was open to learn	I tried to leave the group

When working with a group of teachers and paraprofessionals, I ask the preceding questions. Their responses are shown in Table 3.1.

Examine the lists shown in the table. How do they relate to students in school? Have you seen students in school who feel sick, angry, withdrawn, or hurt? Have you seen students who behave in ways that let you know they do not feel that they belong? On the other hand, have you noticed kids who are engaged, acting like themselves and freely taking risks? As a teacher, I have observed kids who regularly felt connected and those who did not. Helping students feel that they belong is one of the most important jobs of the paraprofessional and teacher.

If a system of special education excludes kids and puts them in separate rooms, hallways, or schools, the children will not behave as well or learn as well. School administrators and teachers all over the country are rethinking the practice of isolating students with disabilities in one room (Causton-Theoharis & Theoharis, 2008; McLeskey & Waldron, 2006). Isolating students in this way causes them to feel different than everyone else and not part of the larger school community. This type of segregation has real consequences for students' self-esteem and ability to learn (Peterson & Hittie, 2002). Inclusive education was built on the foundation that all people have the basic human right to belong.

THE HISTORY OF INCLUSIVE EDUCATION

You might have attended a school in which students with disabilities were educated down the hall, in a separate wing, or in a separate school. You also might have attended a school in which you sat beside kids with disabilities. Your own schooling experience shapes your personal thoughts about inclusive education.

Before 1975, students with disabilities did not have the legal right to attend school. As a result, many students with more significant disabilities were educated in separate schools (paid for by their parents) or institutions or were not educated at all. In 1975, Congress passed the Education for All Handicapped Children Act (PL 94-142), which has since been reauthorized most recently as the Individuals with Disabilities Education Improvement Act (IDEA) of 2004 (PL 108-446). This law, which guarantees all students with disabilities the right to a public education, has proved to be a major accomplishment for people with disabilities and their families. This law ensures that all students with disabilities have access to free appropriate public education (FAPE) in the least restrictive environment (LRE). Each of these terms is defined in the next section.

FREE APPROPRIATE PUBLIC EDUCATION

Free. This term means that all students with disabilities have the right to attend school and that the supports and services necessary to their education will be paid for at the public expense.

Appropriate. This term means that all students with disabilities must be provided the assistive technology, aids, and services that allow them to participate in academic and nonacademic activities.

Public Education. This education is guaranteed in a public school setting.

Least Restrictive Environment

The term that is used to support inclusion in the law is *LRE.* This term is explicitly cited in IDEA 2004, the federal law governing special education. IDEA 2004 stipulates that all students with disabilities have the legal right to be placed in the LRE.

LRE means that, to the maximum extent appropriate, a school district must educate any student with a disability in the regular classroom with appropriate aids and supports, referred to as *supplementary aids and services,* along with the student's peers without disabilities, in the school he or she would attend if the student did not have a disability (IDEA, 2004).

Under LRE, the general education classroom is the first place to be considered for placing a student with a disability before more restrictive options are considered.

What Are Supplementary Aids and Services?

Supplementary aids and services that educators have successfully used include modifications to the regular class curriculum (e.g., preferential seating, use of a computer, taped lectures, reduced seat time), assistance of a teacher with special education training, special education training for the regular teacher, use of computer-assisted devices, provision of notetakers, and changes to materials.

What this means is that educators must utilize all of the possible supplementary aids and services before determining that a student can leave the general education classroom. *Inclusion* is not mentioned in the law, but it is implied, and people use LRE and the multitude of supplementary aides and services to support the idea of inclusion. Therefore, *inclusion* has been defined by scholars.

DEFINING INCLUSIVE EDUCATION

Kunc (1992) defines *inclusive education* as

> the valuing of diversity within the human community. When inclusive education is fully embraced, we abandon the idea that children have to become "normal" in order to contribute to the world . . . . We begin to look beyond typical ways of becoming valued members of the community, and in doing so, begin to realize the achievable goal of providing all children with an authentic sense of belonging. (p. 20)

Udvari-Solner (1997) uses another definition of inclusion:

> Inclusive schooling propels a critique of contemporary school culture and thus, encourages practitioners to reinvent what can be and should be to realize more humane, just and democratic learning communities. Inequities in treatment and educational opportunity are brought to the forefront, thereby fostering attention to human rights, respect for difference and value of diversity. (p. 142)

WHAT DOES INCLUSION LOOK LIKE? INDICATORS OF INCLUSIVE CLASSROOMS

Natural Proportions

In any one classroom, the number of students with disabilities should reflect the natural population of students with disabilities in the school (i.e., no more than 12%). In an inclusive classroom, half the class will not be made up of students with disabilities. Having a greater number of students with disabilities in one setting increases the density of need, making the class more like a special education setting.

Team Teaching

Inclusive classrooms often have two teachers (one general and one special education teacher) with equitable responsibilities for teaching all the students. A paraprofessional often provides additional support to the students who have disabilities while also working with all students in the classroom.

Community Building

In inclusive classrooms, teachers continually use community building to ensure that students feel connected to one another and to their teachers. A common theme in community building is that different people learn in different ways. Community building approaches vary, but, in an inclusive classroom, you might see the day start out with a morning meeting at which students share their feelings or important life events. You might see organized community building in which students learn about each other in systematic ways. For example, the students might be doing a community building exercise called "Homework in a Bag"; in this exercise, each student brings one item that represents him- or herself and shares the item with a small group of other students.

Differentiation

In an inclusive classroom, it is clear that learners of various academic, social, and behavioral levels and needs exist in one space. Therefore, the content is differentiated. Students might work on similar goals, but they do so in different ways. For example, all students might be working on math problems, with some using manipulatives, some drawing out their answers, some checking their problems on calculators, and some using wipe-off markers and white boards.

Kids Do Not Leave to Learn

In an inclusive classroom, you will not have a virtual revolving door of children leaving for specialized instruction. Therapies and services occur within the context of the general education classroom. For example, instead of going to a small room with a speech teacher, a student would work on his or her speech goals while participating in reading instruction.

Engaging Instruction

Inclusive classrooms do not entail a lot of large-group lectures in which the teachers talk and the students passively sit and listen. Learning is exciting in inclusive classrooms. Teachers plan instruction with the range of learning styles in mind. In inclusive classrooms, students experience active learning; they often are up and out of their seats, with partner work and group work used frequently. The content is planned to meet the needs of students to move around, to work with others, to see what they are learning, and to experience their learning.

WHAT DO I NEED TO KNOW ABOUT THE INDIVIDUALIZED EDUCATION PROGRAM?

Every student who receives special education services must have an IEP. A student who has an IEP has already been tested and observed, and a team has determined that the student has a disability. An IEP is a legal plan written by a team of professionals that documents the learning priorities for the school year (Huefner, 2000). This team includes the parent, the student (when appropriate), the general education teacher, the special education teacher, a representative of the school district, and other professionals whose expertise is needed (e.g., psychologist, speech and language clinician, occupational or physical therapist). When writing this document, the team comes together annually to determine and document the student's unique needs and goals regarding his or her participation in the general school curriculum for the upcoming school year. According to the U.S. Department of Education (2004), every IEP must legally include the following information:

- Present levels of performance—this states how a student is performing across all subject areas.

- Measurable goals and objectives—this indicates the annual goals for a student across subject areas.

- Special education and related services—this is the type, level, and amount of service that will be provided by special education staff.

- The extent of participation with children without disabilities—the IEP must note how much time a student spends with general education peers.

- A statement of how the child's progress will be measured—the team needs to describe how often and how a student's progress will be measured.

- Modifications—the student's modifications or adaptations must be listed.

- Participation in statewide tests—the IEP indicates whether the student will participate in statewide tests and, if so, what modifications will be provided.

- Locations of services to be provided—this explains the amount of time students will receive services and the location (e.g., general education classroom).

- Statement of transition services—each student who is at least 16 years of age must have a statement of preparation for adult life.

Paraprofessionals have the legal right to access the IEPs of the students they support. You may be asked to participate in a student's IEP meeting because you can provide important information relevant to the student's educational program. If you are asked to participate, you should meet first with the teacher to discuss your role in the meeting. Even if you do not attend the meeting, you should read the IEPs of the students you support (see Table 3.2). When reading an IEP, the best place to start is with two major sections: 1) the present level of performance and 2) the student's goals and objectives. When reading an IEP, fill out an "IEP at a glance" or a summary listing the goals and objectives and other important information. See Figure 3.1 for a copy of an IEP at a glance. You should understand that the information within the document is confidential and cannot be shared with anyone outside of the child's team. Sharing information about a student is not only disrespectful; it is also potentially illegal (20 U.S.C. § 1412 [a][8]; § 1417 [c]).

Table 3.2.   How to read an individualized education program (IEP)

1. Find the present level of performance. Read it. Now ask yourself . . .	Do I have a clear picture of what this student does well?
	Do I have a clear picture of this student's skills?
	Do I know any strategies that work with this student?
	Do I know what to avoid when working with this student?
2. Find the annual goals. Read each goal. Now ask yourself . . .	Do I have a clear picture of what the student should be able to do by the end of the year?
3. Find the supplementary aids and services (aids, services, and supports to help the student be educated in the general education environment). Read it. Now ask yourself . . .	Do I understand the services and supports that this student needs in regular education environments?
	Do I know who is expected to provide the services or supports?
	If I am expected to provide a service or support, do I know what to do?
4. Find the section on specially designed instruction (direct teaching and services carried out by the special education staff). Read it. Now ask yourself . . .	What specially designed instruction does this student need? Where is the instruction provided? *If* I need to provide practice or support, do I understand what to do?
5. If the student has a behavior intervention plan, find it. Read it. And ask yourself . . .	What are the strategies and techniques that will increase the likelihood that appropriate behaviors will occur? If problem behaviors begin to escalate, how can I redirect the student to more positive behaviors? If the student becomes aggressive, do I know the steps in the response plan to deescalate the situation?
6. Now read the rest of the individualized education plan. Ask yourself . . .	Do I have any questions about this student, his or her needs, or his or her support that I should share with my teaching team?

Any student who has challenging behavior is required to have a behavior intervention plan as part of his or her IEP. This plan includes a functional assessment of the student's behavior and a plan for addressing that student's behavior in positive ways. If a student whom you support has a behavior intervention plan, you are responsible for following the behavior plan as written.

☙ IEP at a Glance ☙

Student _____ Grade _____ Age _____

Date completed _____

Goal _____ | Goal _____
Objectives: | Objectives:

- | -
- | -
- | -
- | -
- | -
- | -
- | -
- | -
- | -

Goal _____ | Goal _____
Objectives: | Objectives:

- | -
- | -
- | -
- | -
- | -
- | -
- | -
- | -
- | -

Goal _____ | Important student information:
Objectives: |

- | -
- | -
- | -
- | -
- | -
- | -
- | -
- | -
- | -

Figure 3.1.   An individualized education program (IEP) at a glance.

COMMONLY ASKED
QUESTIONS ABOUT INCLUSIVE EDUCATION

Q. Is inclusive education really best for this kid?

A. This is a common question asked by teachers and paraprofessionals alike. Our job is to figure out how to make the general education environment suitable to the student's needs.

Q. I do not think my student is getting anything out of this class. What should I do?

A. If you don't think a student is gaining anything from the class curriculum, it is the teacher's responsibility (with your support) to modify or adapt the content so that the student can benefit from the instruction. Sometimes, the goals of the lesson are not easy to see. In such cases, initiate a discussion with the teacher(s) about what the expected goals of the lesson are (the student might be working on social goals, occupational therapy goals, or just being present to learn the content).

Q. When should I take a student out of the classroom?

A. Some students make noises during class or distract other students. Most of these behaviors are attempts to communicate or the results of disabilities. There are significant problems with reacting by removing a child. Think how you would feel if you were removed from a learning environment; you might feel angry, humiliated, or embarrassed. Students have the same reaction. Especially if such actions are used continually, a student might begin to feel that something is wrong with him or her. Removing a student can create an environment that feels unsafe. Every student has the right to an education in the general education classroom, and it is not your decision to remove anyone. If a student is having behavioral issues, the team of teachers has the responsibility to identify and help the student manage the behavior within the context of the classroom. Provide an option for the student to identify when he or she might need a break. Escorting a student out of a room without his or her permission is not an effective solution.

Q. What could I do instead of removing a student?

A. Remove yourself. Sometimes, switching adults or backing away is the best solution if you are having a difficult time with a student. Help students engage in a different way. Give the student a choice at that moment (e.g., a choice of materials, a choice of whom to work with). See removal as the last resort. Chapter 8 presents many more ideas.

Q. Will other kids tease students with disabilities?

A. If you see or hear about teasing, you must deal with or report it. Teasing should not be seen as an inevitable consequence of inclusion. In fact, in inclusive settings, teasing often is not an issue, but if it becomes one, it must be dealt with directly and swiftly. No one has to endure teasing.

Q.   Is inclusion really the law?

A.   IDEA 2004 does not use the term *inclusion*. Nonetheless, the law stipulates that all students must be placed in the LRE. The first consideration must be the general education setting, and schools must prove that they have attempted to teach all children in the general education setting with appropriate supplementary aids and services before considering placement in more restrictive settings.

CONCLUSION

Schools today are becoming increasingly inclusive. Therefore, paraprofessionals working in inclusive settings need to understand the rationale for inclusive schooling, the history of inclusive schooling, major concepts in inclusive schooling, indicators of inclusion, and the concept of the IEP as a framework to most fully support students in inclusive settings. You will not be expected to do this alone; you will be part of a team. The next chapter focuses on how you fit into a collaborative team that will work to educate all students.

NOTES

_____

_____

_____

_____

_____

_____

_____

_____

_____

_____

_____

_____

_____

_____

_____

_____

_____

_____

_____

_____

_____

_____

_____

_____

4

Collaborating with Others

Working within a Team

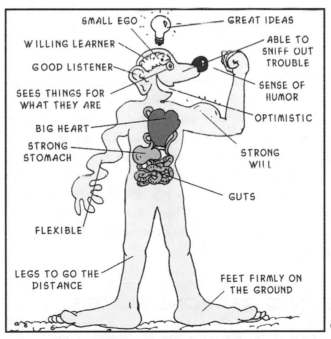

SMALL EGO

GREAT IDEAS

WILLING LEARNER

ABLE TO SNIFF OUT TROUBLE

GOOD LISTENER

SENSE OF HUMOR

SEES THINGS FOR WHAT THEY ARE

OPTIMISTIC

BIG HEART

STRONG STOMACH

STRONG WILL

GUTS

FLEXIBLE

LEGS TO GO THE DISTANCE

FEET FIRMLY ON THE GROUND

ANATOMY OF AN EFFECTIVE TEAM MEMBER

Throughout an entire school day, I collaborate and work with dozens of people. I work closely with my fourth-grade team, the [general education] teacher, the special education teacher, and the program assistant. I also work with the speech and language clinician, the psychologist, the occupational therapist, the physical therapist, and, of course, I work closely with all of the special area teachers: music, art, physical education. Across the day, I have hundreds of interactions with adults. Sometimes that is the most challenging part of my job.
—Ted (paraprofessional)

We've each been invited to this present moment by design. Our lives are joined together like the tiles of a mosaic; none of us contributes the whole of the picture, but each of us is necessary for its completion.
—Casey & Vanceburg (1996)

All students in a classroom community can benefit from a team of educators, which includes paraprofessionals and teachers working together in ways that promote meaningful learning and a sense of belonging for all students. In an inclusive classroom, the supporting adults are like tiles of a mosaic. Each person is an important contributor to the larger picture. In today's inclusive classrooms, it is quite common for general education teachers and special education teachers to work alongside paraprofessionals. This chapter provides information and tools that will enable paraprofessionals to engage in effective collaboration. To achieve this, the resources available are maximized to ensure all students' participation and learning. In some cases, however, teachers and paraprofessionals work in isolation. Some common problems that arise from this are that paraprofessionals, who have unclear roles in the classroom, feel devalued and are left alone to determine student expectations and classroom rules. They often need information about students and strategies.

This chapter will help you to see your role as a member of the larger teaching team and to address the roles and responsibilities of each team member. I propose general ways to communicate with the whole teaching team, cosupporting structures, and strategies for handling conflict. Then, I discuss some of the ethical considerations of confidentiality inherent in the job of the paraprofessional. Finally, I address commonly asked questions about collaboration.

ROLES AND RESPONSIBILITIES

Roles and responsibilities of school staff vary among schools, districts, and even states. Nonetheless, despite these variations, there are generally accepted roles and responsibilities that hold true from school to school. The next section provides some general guidelines for how school personnel can work effectively as a team to meet the needs of all students together.

The Teaching Team

The Paraprofessional   As discussed in Chapter 1, paraprofessionals are expected to perform many different tasks. Supporting students and supporting instruction are the focus of the work of paraprofessionals. The following is an example of a job description taken from a district in the Midwest, although your job description may differ. See your building principal or union representative to obtain a copy of your official job description.

> Under the supervision of the building principal the paraprofessional reviews and reinforces instruction to Pre K-12 students with a variety of disabilities in integrated school, community and vocational settings. (Madison Public Schools, 2007)

Here are some examples of the essential functions of paraprofessionals:

- Work with a wide range of students with cognitive disabilities and/or multiple disabilities including transfers, applying adaptive devices, tube feedings, diapering, bathroom assistance, and mobility training.

- Maintain records, including data collection (i.e., charting seizure activities).

- Provide instructional reinforcement to students in the classroom and at community-based sites under the direction of a teacher.

- Assist students individually and in small groups with academic and recreational programming under a teacher's direction.

- Monitor and manage student behavior consistent with behavior management programs.

- Develop social skills under a teacher's direction.

- Diffuse conflict situations.

- Perform other related duties as assigned.

The Special Educator   By definition, a special educator has earned a college degree in teaching. A special educator is partly responsible for designing each student's individualized education program (IEP). Each year, a team of teachers and parents determines each student's goals and objectives and the appropriate special education services. The special education teacher helps to ensure that the goals and objectives on each student's IEP are met. In collaboration with general education teachers and support staff, the special education teacher is responsible for helping to differentiate curricula and instruction and provides and recommends modifications and adaptations that would be appropriate for each student. Special education teachers are also responsible for solving problems that arise in the classroom, evaluating each student's services, and communicating student progress to the team.

The General Educator   A general educator usually can be expected to educate the students in his or her class. A general educator plans lessons, teaches these lessons, and assesses each student's skill. A general educator is responsible not only for each student with an IEP but also for all of the students who do not have disabilities. Typically, a general educator is considered the content expert for the particular grade level being taught.

The Family   Family members are undoubtedly the most important people in a child's life. With the reauthorization of the Individuals with Disabilities Education Improvement Act of 2004 (PL 108-446), parents/guardians became equal members of students' IEP teams. Parents/guardians are expected to be active members of their children's educations because they know their children better than anyone else. Teachers and paraprofessionals can help parents play active roles by communicating all that happens in the school setting and, further, by listening closely to the wishes and concerns of family members.

Occupational Therapists   For a student who works with an occupational therapist, the student's disability necessitates support in daily life skills. The therapist may evaluate the student's needs, provide therapy, modify classroom equipment, and generally help the student participate as fully as possible in school programs and activities. A therapist may work with children individually or lead small groups. Therapists also may consult with teachers and paraprofessionals to help students meet their goals within the context of general education settings. Specific types of therapies may include help with handwriting, computer work, fostering social play, teaching life skills such as getting dressed, or eating with utensils. The difference between the role of occupational therapist and physical therapist can be confusing; in general occupational therapists work more with fine motor skills, and physical therapists work more with gross motor skills.

Physical Therapists   Physical therapy, like occupational therapy, is a related service and is provided by a qualified and licensed physical therapist. Physical therapists address areas such as gross motor development skills, orthopedic concerns, mobility, adaptive equipment, positioning needs, and other functional skills that may interfere with students' educational performance. Similar to an occupational therapist, a physical therapist either works with individual students or leads small groups. Physical therapists also consult with teachers and paraprofessionals. Specific types of therapies include practice walking up and down stairs safely, stretching the body after sitting in a wheelchair, or help performing other physical activities.

Speech and Language Therapists   Speech and language therapists (sometimes called speech pathologists, or SLPs) help students with communication and with all of the skills required to communicate effectively. These skills include all issues related to language, the voice, swallowing, and fluency. Some students who work with speech and language therapists have issues with stuttering. Others work on understanding and producing language. In schools, speech-language therapists collaborate with teaching teams to support classroom activities and effective communication.

Psychologists   The goals of school psychologists are to help children and youth succeed academically, socially, and emotionally. School psychologists work closely with teaching teams to create healthy and safe learning environments and to strengthen connections between each student's home and school. Psychologists assess students and are often involved in standardized testing to determine whether a student qualifies as having a disability. Psychologists also work directly with others on teaching teams by helping to problem solve and, at times, provide direct support services to students.

Social Workers   Like psychologists, school social workers help provide links connecting each student's home, school, and community. The services provided by social workers are intended to help enable students and families to overcome problems that may impede learning. School social workers provide individual and group counseling, consult with teachers, and teach or encourage social skills. They collaborate with community agencies and provide service coordination for students who require many different agencies or services.

Vision Teachers/Audiologists   Vision teachers support students who have visual impairments or blindness. Vision teachers typically work with classroom teachers to make modifications and adaptations to the curricula. They also help provide needed equipment (e.g., magnifiers and computer equipment). Audiologists typically work with students who have hearing impairments, providing amplification systems and sign language interpreters for students who are deaf.

HOW DO ALL THESE PEOPLE WORK TOGETHER?

Every school differs, but one thing is certain: All the adults on a teaching team must work together for the purpose of promoting student growth. One example of effective collaboration involves a seventh-grade team.

∙∙∙∙∙∙∙∙∙∙

This team involves all of the staff who support Adam, a student with autism and a visual impairment. The core team of people supporting Adam in English class includes the English teacher, the vision teacher, the special education teacher, and a paraprofessional. This team meets monthly to discuss Adam's support in English class. Every week, the vision teacher and the English teacher meet with the paraprofessional to create enlarged materials for upcoming units of study. In addition, the special education teacher and the English teacher plan lessons together with Adam in mind so that each lesson is designed to meet Adam's needs. For example, they planned a unit using a book from the Harry Potter series. In addition to having the paraprofessional enlarge the text in the packet of information, the teacher decided to have the entire class listen to an audio version of the book instead of reading silently. The paraprofessional receives written plans each day. This plan outlines the anticipated type and level of support that Adam needs during each activity.

· · · · · · · · · ·

GUIDING QUESTIONS FOR TEAMS TO DISCUSS

Getting to know your teammates on a personal level is necessary for real and true collaboration to occur. Some questions that will help you as you sit down with a teacher or group of teachers are listed in this section. You may approach this list as some simple suggestions, or you may decide to go through each question with your team.

Work Styles

- Are you a morning or afternoon person?

- How direct are you?

- Do you like to do several things at once, or do you prefer doing one thing at a time?

- How do you prefer to give feedback to others on the team?

- What do you consider your strengths and weaknesses when working in a team situation?

Philosophy

- To me, advanced planning means . . .

- All kids learn best when . . .

- In general, I think the best way to deal with challenging behavior is . . .

- In general, I think it is important to increase student independence by . . .

- I think our team relationship needs to be . . .

Logistics

- How should we communicate about students' history and progress?
- How should we communicate about our roles and responsibilities?
- How and when should we communicate about lessons and modifications?
- If I do not know an answer in class, should I direct the student to you?
- Do we meet often enough? If not, when should we meet?
- How do we communicate with the families? What is each person's role in this?
- Are there other logistical concerns?

Questions for the Family

- How would you like to communicate about your child's progress?

- If we are using a communication notebook or e-mail, how often would you like to hear from the school?
- Are there things you are especially interested in hearing about?

After having personal discussions using these questions as a guide, teams are better able to negotiate the logistical and philosophical components of teamwork, allowing team members to feel more comfortable in knowing the roles and expectations within the classroom setting. The next section describes some coteaching and cosupporting arrangements that should give further clarity to the collaborative work of adults in the classroom.

COSUPPORTING ARRANGEMENTS

Because paraprofessionals generally do not introduce or teach new content, I have adapted some coteaching arrangements from Friend & Reising (1993) and have created some cosupporting arrangements.

One Teach–One Observe

While the teacher is teaching, you might observe and take data on student performance. You also could collect information on the students' behavior.

One Teach–One Support

While the teacher is instructing in the large group, you might provide support to students in the class. You could answer questions or bring students back to attention. You also could write or draw examples on the chalkboard. If a student whom you support has significant needs (e.g., a seizure disorder or medical needs that require proximity), you will want to remain close to the student. But, for the most part, you should help all students even if you have been assigned to work only with one.

Station Facilitation

It is perfectly fine for a paraprofessional to run a small group or a station. It is important, however, for paraprofessionals first to receive instructions on how to run these stations (preferably in the form of a lesson plan or task card). A paraprofessional should, at minimum, know the goal of the station, how to instruct the students, and what modifications or adaptations should be used with individual students.

Table 4.1. Ideas for providing engaged support

If the teacher is doing this:	You can be doing this:
Lecturing	Modeling note taking on the board, drawing the ideas on the board, or taking notes on the overhead
Taking attendance	Collecting and reviewing homework
Giving directions	Writing the directions on the board so all students have a place to look for the visual cues
Providing large-group instruction	Collecting data on student behavior or engagement, or making modifications for an upcoming lesson
Giving a test	Reading the test to students who prefer to have the test read to them
Facilitating stations or small groups	Also facilitating stations or groups
Facilitating sustained, silent reading	Reading aloud quietly with a small group
Teaching a new concept	Providing visuals or models to enhance the whole group's understanding
Reteaching or preteaching with a small group	Monitoring the large group as they work independently

Source: Murawski and Dieker (2004).

Cosupport

Another common type of support is called *cosupport.* While the teacher is leading the large group, you can ask clarifying questions or provide examples. Table 4.1 shows some types of cosupport you might provide in different situations, as suggested by Murawski and Dieker (2004).

WHAT IF CONFLICT ARISES?

The kids aren't the hard part of my job. It is working with other adults that I find challenging.

—Pam (paraprofessional)

Ideal team functioning is like a well-oiled machine in which each cog runs continually and smoothly, each harmoniously performing an individual function for the good of the entire machine. However, team functioning does not always feel this smooth. Conflicts among adults do arise.

The Bonner Foundation, a nonprofit education organization, has suggested eight steps for conflict resolution. *Conflict* is defined as "a mental or physical disagreement in which people's values or needs are in opposition to each or they think that they are opposed" (Bonner Foundation, 2008). The Bonner Foundation's suggestions for handling conflicts are listed here:

1. Identify positions ("what are they saying") of each side of the people in conflict. Write down your perspective and the other person's perspective.

2. Learn more about true needs and desires behind each side. Write down your beliefs about the other person's needs and desires. Write down your own needs and desires.

3. Ask clarifying questions for more information. Ask the other person, "Why do you feel the way you do?" "What do you feel you need in this situation?" Reframe the problem into a question.

4. Brainstorm possible solutions. Without judging the ideas, write down as many ideas as you can.

5. Discuss how each solution would affect each side, and figure out possible compromises. Talk through each of the potential solutions. Discuss which ones would work and would not work, from your perspective and from the other person's perspective. Generate more ideas, if necessary.

6. Agree on a solution. Determine which solution would work the best for both of you. Write out a plan for carrying out the solution and determine how long you plan to implement the solution.

7. Implement solutions. Give your idea a try for the determined amount of time.

8. Reevaluate solutions, if necessary. Come back together to discuss the solution and what is working/not working about this solution. Continue the process as necessary.

MAKING THE TIME TO COMMUNICATE

I have spoken with hundreds of paraprofessionals across the country, and one of the most common problems they mention involves not having enough time to communicate or collaborate with the teachers with whom they work. Different teaching teams have solved this problem by using several different strategies. Each strategy is described in the following list. Examine each strategy and see whether it will help your team communicate more regularly and more effectively. The following strategies have been successfully used to carve out more meeting time:

- *Video or independent work time*—Create a weekly meeting time during which students are expected to watch instructional videos or to work independently for 15 minutes. Allow them to watch or work independently while the team meets.

- *Use a parent volunteer*—As a parent volunteer reads a book to the students or leads a review game, meet together for 15 minutes.

- *Use another teacher team*—Put two classrooms together for a half-hour each week for a certain portion of the curriculum or community-building activities. One teaching team supervises the students while the other team meets. The teams then switch.

- *Meet during specials time*—Ask the specials teachers whether their classes have any 15-minute periods that might not require paraprofessional support. Use that time to meet together.

- *Meet before or after school time*—Take 15 minutes before or after school to have a "sacred" meeting time for teaching teams.

If you simply cannot use any of these strategies to elicit more face-to-face meeting times, some teams have come up with alternatives to meeting face-to-face.

- *Communication notebook*—Establish a notebook that all members of the team read and respond to each day. Team members can write questions in the notebook and obtain responses. Notebooks also can be used to discuss schedules or student-specific information.

- *E-mail*—E-mail can be substituted for the communication notebook; team members can contact each other with questions, comments, or schedule changes.

- *Mailbox*—Use a mailbox in the classroom for each staff member. Direct all notes or general information to that place.

- *Proofread*—As notes are written that go home to the students' parents, have the teaching team proofread each of the notes. This way, not only are the notes proofread, but everyone receives all of the necessary information.

- *Lesson plan sharing*—Keep lesson plans out and accessible to all members of the team. Use the notes to communicate about upcoming content. Ask the person who writes the plans to delineate each team member's role for each lesson.

ETHICAL CONSIDERATIONS: CONFIDENTIALITY

Confidentiality is one of the most crucial aspects of the job of a paraprofessional. You are an ambassador of the school district. As you do your job, you will have to be careful when others ask questions about school situations. Many parents and community members might ask for details about student behavior, disability, or activities. Think of ways to deflect potentially inappropriate personal questions. For example, a parent approaches you and says, "I notice you work with Lucy. Why does she need a walker?" What would you say in response? Consider saying something such as, "I am sorry, but school confidentiality does not allow me to talk about that." Then, direct the parent to someone with whom he or she can talk: "Feel free to ask [general education teacher, special education teacher, or principal]."

COMMONLY ASKED QUESTIONS ABOUT COLLABORATION

Q. I am not sure what I am supposed to be doing in art class. We (the art teacher and I) have never talked, so mostly I just sit and support two students. What should I do?

A. Set up a time to meet with the art teacher. Ask questions such as, "How can I be most useful to the students in this class?" "When you are giving directions, how can I best support you?" "When the students are working on a project, what would you like me to do, and what would you like me not to do?" These kinds of conversations are crucial in any classroom in which you will be providing support.

Q. I have read about common support arrangements, but we do not use any of them; instead, I just sit and support or walk around and support. How can I suggest that we use these strategies?

A. Show your teacher the arrangements. Begin a conversation asking whether the arrangements might be useful to your team.

Q. What if I feel uncomfortable with a role I have been assigned?

A. Communicate your concerns to your teaching team. The role might not have to be changed; it could be shared. If you feel you are being asked to do something outside the scope of your job, talk to the teaching team first and then to your principal or director of special education.

Q. What is confidential about my job?

A. First, check to see what is outlined in your school policy and what your team deems confidential. Then, consider this question: If this were me, or my child, would I want this information shared with others? Err on the side of maintaining confidentiality.

Q. What do I do on the spot when someone asks me something that is confidential?

A. Prepare and practice catch phrases in advance, such as "Mrs. Keen would be the person to ask."

CONCLUSION

Working as a team member and within a school setting can be challenging, but it also can be rewarding. Understanding each team member's roles, including your own, can bring clarity to your work. Learning more information about each of your teammates is essential to building trust among your team. Further, using common cosupporting arrangements can clarify specific roles and responsibilities within the classroom. Communication is key: The more effectively you communicate and solve conflicts as you work together, the better your team will function, enabling you to deliver more seamless support to students. The next chapter focuses on how to rethink students in terms of their strengths, gifts, and talents so that they can reach their full academic potential.

NOTES

_____
_____
_____
_____
_____
_____
_____
_____
_____
_____
_____
_____
_____
_____
_____
_____
_____

5

Rethinking Students

Presuming Competence

THE MOST APPROPRIATE LABEL IS
USUALLY THE ONE PEOPLE'S PARENTS
HAVE GIVEN THEM.

I have been a paraprofessional for 23 years. The biggest surprise to me is that these students are really smart. When I began working . . . we would have them practice writing their name and address every day, they would work on matching colors to these plastic bears—and the kids hated doing the same things over and over.

Then we got a new teacher, and things changed! We were now expected to take these kids into classrooms like algebra and physics. I thought [the teacher] was crazy (laughing) . . . But, I will never forget the day I was supporting Daniel. I gave him the calculator to figure out the problem . . . and it was a hard problem too. He pushed the calculator away, refusing to use it, and he wrote the answer down. I checked it. He was right! It made me want to cry. Who knows what we have done to kids like Daniel in the past, and who knows just what kids like Daniel can do!?

—Chantel (paraprofessional)

When I approach a child, [s]he inspires in me two sentiments: tenderness for what [s]he is, and respect for what [s]he may become.

—Louis Pasteur (Institut Pasteur, n.d.)

This chapter introduces the concept of *rethinking students*. Rethinking a student entails getting to know about the student and then reflecting on how you see, treat, and work with him or her. First, I discuss how to describe students to others through student strengths and multiple intelligences. Then, I describe the concept of presumption of competence and using age-appropriate and person-first language. (Please see Table 5.3 for examples of person-first language.)

STUDENT DESCRIPTIONS

Shawntell Strully is a 22-year-old who lives in her own home with roommates, attends classes at Colorado State University, volunteers on campus, travels during spring break, gets around in her own car, has her own interests, likes and desires, has a boyfriend, and speaks out on issues of concern to her.

Shawntell Strully is 22 years old, is severely/profoundly mentally retarded, is hearing impaired, visually impaired, has cerebral palsy, has a seizure disorder, does not chew her food (and sometimes chokes), is not toilet trained, has no verbal communication, has no reliable communication system, and has a developmental age of 17–24 months. (Strully & Strully, 1996, pp. 144–145)

These two radically different descriptions of Shawntell come from two different groups of people. The first description comes from her parents. The second comes from her teachers and other school support personnel. Although not all teachers would describe Shawntell in these ways, this is how her team described her. It is surprising to compare these statements side-by-side. The stark contrast raises the question of how the same person can be described in such disparate ways.

The principal reason for these radically different descriptions is that each group of people looks for different things and approaches Shawntell from a different perspective. Shawntell's parents know her deeply. They have spent a great deal of time with her, know her intimately, and understand her as a person who has wide interests and capabilities. Their description of her cites her interests, gifts, and talents. Conversely, the description generated by Shawntell's teachers reflects a more distant understanding of her; it is a cold, clinical account that focuses exclusively on her impairments.

As a paraprofessional working with students with disabilities, you will hear impairment-driven descriptions of students, and, thus, you will need to work to understand these students through their strengths, gifts, and talents. You may read a student's individualized education program, and it might abound with phrases such as *mental age of 2, phobic,* or *aggressive.* Reading those descriptors, you will need to realize that you are getting only one perspective on the student. Get to know the student yourself, and work to learn about what he or she can do. Hopefully, your descriptions of a student would look much closer to the parents' perspective on Shawntell than that of the teachers.

BEGIN WITH STRENGTHS

I was talking with Beth, a paraprofessional, and I asked her to describe Iris, a student whom she was supporting. She described Iris as autistic, sensitive, loud, sometimes sweet, and nonverbal. These descriptions speak to Beth's own beliefs about the student. On a separate piece of paper, write down the first 10 descriptors that come to mind when *you* think of an individual student. Now, look over the list. Were your descriptors positive, negative, or a combination?

Your beliefs about a student will impact how you support and work with that student. For example, if you believe a student is lazy or defiant, you will approach him or her in a different way than you will if you believe that child is motivated or cooperative. You can alter your beliefs about students by spending some time rethinking them. Reframing your conceptions of students in more positive ways creates opportunities for growth.

Consider the work of educational researcher Thomas Armstrong (2000a, 2000b) on using Multiple Intelligence theory in the classroom. Armstrong recommended that education professionals purposefully rethink the ways they describe students. By changing their language, people will begin to change their impressions. Armstrong emphasized that all behavior is part of the human experience and that behavior is based on a multitude of influences (environment, sense of safety, personal well-being). Armstrong has proposed that instead of considering a child *learning disabled,* people see the child as *learning differently.* Table 5.1 lists further suggestions for describing students.

What would happen if all education professionals changed how they viewed and spoke about students? What if every student were viewed as a capable learner? One of the best ways to think about the students whom you support is to look at the child through the lens of his or her strengths. Ask yourself the following questions: "What

Table 5.1. Turning lead into gold

A child who is judged to be	Can also be considered
Learning disabled	Learning differently
Hyperactive	Kinesthetic
Impulsive	Spontaneous
ADD/ADHD	A bodily-kinesthetic learner
Dyslexic	A spatial learner
Aggressive	Assertive
Plodding	Thorough
Lazy	Relaxed
Immature	Late blooming
Phobic	Cautious
Scattered	Divergent
Daydreaming	Imaginative
Irritable	Sensitive
Perseverative	Persistent

Key: ADD, attention deficit disorder; ADHD, attention-deficit/hyperactivity disorder.

From Table 10-1: Turning lead into gold," from IN THEIR OWN WAY by Thomas Armstrong, copyright © 1988 by Thomas Armstrong. Used by permission of Jeremy P. Tarcher, an imprint of Penguin Group (USA) Inc..

can this student do?" "What are this person's strengths?" "How would a parent who deeply loves this student speak about him or her?" Now, return to your list and take a moment to develop a list of strengths, gifts, and interests.

During a workshop with a group of teachers and paraprofessionals, Kathy, a paraprofessional, did just that. First, she wrote a list of descriptors. Then, after spending some time rethinking the student, she came up with a completely different list. She had originally described the student, Brian, as "lazy, smart, sneaky, a liar, cute, cunning, and mean (at times)." After talking about viewing students differently, she got a new piece of paper. She wrote, "relaxed, intelligent, good in math, cute, needs some support with peer relationships, a great sense of humor, and a beautiful smile." I asked Kathy whether this still accurately described Brian. She said that the second list was a much *more* accurate description of him.

MULTIPLE INTELLIGENCES

There is a pervasive myth in education that some people are smart and that others are not. *Intelligence, academic potential,* and *competence* are words often used to describe "smartness." In education, this belief can be seen best through the system of labeling

Table 5.2. A guide to supporting through multiple intelligences

Intelligence	Which means	So support using
Verbal/linguistic intelligence	Good with words and language, written and spoken	Jokes, speeches, readings, stories, essays, the Internet, books, biographies
Logical mathematical intelligence	Preference for reasoning, numbers, and patterns	Mazes, puzzles, timelines, analogies, formulas, calculations, codes, games, probabilities
Spatial intelligence	Ability to visualize an object or to create mental images or pictures	Mosaics, drawings, illustrations, models, maps, videos, posters
Bodily kinesthetic intelligence	Knowledge or wisdom of the body and movement	Role-playing, skits, facial expressions, experiments, field trips, sports, games
Musical intelligence	Ability to recognize tonal patterns including sensitivity to rhythms or beats	Performances, songs, instruments, rhythms, compositions, melodies, raps, jingles, choral readings
Interpersonal intelligence	Good with person-to-person interactions and relationships	Group projects, group tasks, observation dialogs, conversation, debate, games, interviews
Intrapersonal intelligence	Knowledge of an inner-state of being; effective and aware	Journals, meditation, self-assessment, recording, creative expression, goal setting, affirmation, poetry
Naturalistic intelligence	Knowledge of the outside world (e.g., plants, animals, weather patterns)	Field trips, observation, nature walks, forecasting, star gazing, fishing, exploring, categorizing, collecting, identifying

Sources: Gardner (1993); Armstrong (2000a, 2000b).

people with disabilities. A clear example is IQ testing. Students take IQ tests, and if a student's IQ score falls below 70 and he or she has other issues with functional skills, the student receives the label of mental retardation. Howard Gardner challenged the way psychologists and educators defined *intelligences* and offered a different way to look at intelligence. He used the term *multiple intelligences* (Gardner, 1993).

Gardner viewed each of the multiple intelligences as a capacity that is inherent in the human brain and that is developed and expressed in social and cultural contexts. Instead of viewing intelligence as a fixed number on an aptitude test, Gardner argued that every person, regardless of disability label, is smart in different ways. All of the eight intelligences are described in Table 5.2. I have also added a column entitled "So support using," which might help you think of the students you support. If you work with a student who prefers to learn in a certain intelligence area or who is strong in a certain area, consider some of the suggested activities and teaching styles.

PRESUME COMPETENCE

In the school setting, assumptions about students can affect their education. Take Sue Rubin, for instance.

....

Sue, a student with autism, had no formal way of communicating until she was 13 years old. Before that time, she had been treated and educated as if she had a mental age of 2 years old. Mental age is often based on a person's score on an IQ test. For example, if a 14-year-old girl's score on an IQ were the score of a "typical" or "normal" 3-year-old, she would be labeled as having the mental age of a 3-year-old. This is not a useful way to think about intelligence. When Sue acquired a form of communication called facili-tated communication, *those long-held assumptions were no longer valid. People began to realize that she was very smart. She subsequently took advanced placement classes all through her high school career, and she is now in college.* (Biklen, 2005; Rubin, 2003)

....

Because education professionals have no real way of determining what a student understands, they should presume that every student is competent or capable. Anne Donnellan uses the term *least dangerous assumption* to describe this idea: "Least dangerous assumption states that in the absence of absolute evidence, it is essential to make the assumption that, if proven to be false, would be least dangerous to the individual" (Donnellan, 1984, p. 24). In other words, it is better to presume that students are competent and that they can learn than to expect that they cannot learn.

Biklen and Burke (2006) have described this idea of presuming competence by explaining that outside observers (e.g., teachers, parents, paraprofessionals) have a choice: They can determine either that a person is competent or incompetent. The presumption of competence recognizes that no one can definitively know another person's thinking unless the other person can (accurately) reveal it. As Biklen and Burke put it, "Presuming competence refuses to limit opportunity . . . it casts the teachers, parents, and others in the role of finding ways to support the person to demonstrate his or her agency" (p. 167).

AGE-APPROPRIATE LANGUAGE

There is a tendency for people to speak down to individuals with disabilities (as if they were younger than they actually are) because of assumptions that people with disabilities are at younger developmental levels. For example, I have heard a paraprofessional ask a high school student, "Do you have to use the potty?" You would not ask a high school student who did not have a disability that same question in that same way. I also have overheard someone describe a young man with Down syndrome who attends college as "a real cutie." Individuals with disabilities should be described in accordance with their actual chronological ages.

Paraprofessionals should treat and work with students in age-appropriate ways. I once witnessed a paraprofessional holding hands with a sixth-grade student in the hall. I doubt that the paraprofessional would have thought it appropriate to hold the hand of a sixth-grade student who did not have a disability. For that very reason, it is inappropriate to hold any student's hand. This same logic holds true for having students sit on your lap, play with age-inappropriate toys, sing age-inappropriate songs, and so forth. Ask yourself how you would talk to or work with the student if she or he did not have a disability, and proceed in that manner.

PERSON-FIRST LANGUAGE

If thoughts corrupt language, language can also corrupt thought.
—George Orwell (1981)

When describing, speaking, or writing respectfully about people who have disabilities, many people use a common language. It is called *person-first language.* The concept of person-first language is simple.

The Same as Anyone Else

Think first about how you might introduce someone who does not have a disability. You might use the person's name, say how you know him or her, or describe what he or she does. The same is true for individuals with disabilities. Instead of saying, "Chelsea who has Down syndrome," you might say, "Chelsea who is in my fourth-grade class." No one should be identified by one aspect of who he or she is (especially if that aspect represents a difficulty or struggle for someone). For example, I would not want anyone to introduce me by saying, "This is Julie, who struggled with statistics." The same is true when talking about a person with a disability. Ask yourself why you would need to mention that the person has a disability.

Words are powerful. The ways we talk about and describe people with disabilities do not just affect our beliefs and interactions with our students; they also provide models for others who hear these descriptions.

If your own child broke his arm, would you introduce him to someone new as "my broken-armed child"? If one of the students in the school had cancer, would you expect to hear a teacher state, "She is my cancerous student"? Of course not. No one should feel ashamed about having a broken arm or having cancer, but a broken bone or malfunctioning cells do not define a person. Would *you* like to be known for your medical history?

Avoid the Label

The same is true for people with disabilities. Yet, students with disabilities are invariably described with labels instead of person-first language. Have you ever heard phrases such as *the learning-disabled student, the autistic boy, that Downs child, the resource room kids,* or *the inclusion kids?*

   It is important to understand the preferences of people with disabilities regarding how they would like others to speak about them. The following guidelines listed in Table 5.3 come from several different self-advocacy groups (disabilityisnatural.com and TASH).

Table 5.3.   Examples of person-first language

Say	Instead of	Because
People with disabilities	The disabled or handicapped	Place emphasis on the person.
People without disabilities	Normal/healthy/ typical	These words (e.g., *abnormal, unhealthy, atypical*) assume the opposite for students with disabilities.
Ella, the fourth-grade student	Ella, the student with Down syndrome	Omit the label whenever possible; it is most often not relevant.
Communicates with her eyes/device, and so forth	Is nonverbal	Focus on strengths.
Uses a wheelchair	Is confined to a wheelchair	Use possessive language to refer to assistive technologies; the nonpreferred language implies the person is "stuck."
Accessible parking spot	Handicapped parking spot	Accurate representation
Beth has autism.	Beth is autistic.	Emphasize that disability is one attribute—not a defining characteristic.
Gail has a learning disability.	Gail is learning disabled.	Emphasize that disability is one attribute—not a defining characteristic.
Jeff has a cognitive disability.	Jeff is retarded.	Emphasize that disability is one attribute—not a defining characteristic. Also, *cognitive disability* is a preferred term.
Ben receives special education services.	Ben is in special education.	Special education is a service, not a place.
The student who is blind	The blind student	Place the person before the disability.
Denis writes using the computer.	Denis can't write with a pencil.	Focus on strengths.
Needs a magnifier, laptop, or cane	Problems with vision; can't write or walk	Focus on needs, not problems.

Source: Snow (2008).

COMMONLY ASKED
QUESTIONS ABOUT STUDENTS

Q. What if a student prefers an age-inappropriate toy or game?

A. Often, people with disabilities have been treated as if they were younger than they are. As a result, they have been exposed to cartoons, dolls, or games to which their same-age peers have not been exposed; their peers are not likely to think these activities are cool. One option, then, is to expose the student to more age-appropriate music and activities.

Q. Are there any exceptions to person-first language?

A. Yes, people who are deaf often prefer the term *deaf* instead of *person with deafness.* A group called Deaf First suggests that deafness is a major component of identity, and this group prefers disability-first language. Some people with autism prefer to be called *autistic,* and some use insider language such as *autie* to describe themselves. It is not accurate to say that all people with disabilities prefer one way over another. Person-first language serves as a helpful guideline because many advocacy groups consider it a respectful way to refer to people.

Q. I do not think the student I work with is smart. This student has a label of mental retardation. How can I presume competence?

A. This person may not perform well on standardized tests of intelligence. However, your responsibility when working with this student is to identify the student's strengths. Keep those strengths in mind. Every person is intelligent in different ways.

CONCLUSION

Remember, these labels are not accurate descriptors of people. Children who have disabilities are unique individuals with unlimited potential, just like everyone else (Snow, 2008). This recognition is not only about having a good attitude or believing that all students are smart; it also will allow you to treat, support, and work with all students in ways that promote dignity and respect. In the next chapter, I discuss how the ideas of dignity and respect can help facilitate social relationships.

NOTES

6

Providing
Social Supports

Standing Back

JOEY NOTICED A MYSTERIOUS FORCE FIELD
AROUND HIS ASSISTANT THAT CHILDREN
COULD NOT BREAK THROUGH.

··········

Seth sits down at the lunch table all by himself. Five minutes later, a few students sit at the same table. The distance between the other students and Seth makes it clear that they are not sitting with him. Seth quietly eats his lunch. Chewing carefully and using his napkin, Seth finishes his lunch and slowly packs up his belongings. He looks over at the other students. They are engaged in a conversation about their soccer team. No one says a word to Seth during lunch, and he does not talk with anyone during the entire lunch period. He puts his head down on his arm and closely examines the threads on his sweatshirt until the bell rings to indicate that lunch is over. Seth stands up and walks over to Judy, the paraprofessional who will walk him to his next class.

··········

There are kids like Seth at every school and in many classrooms. Often, when a student has a disability or receives support from a paraprofessional, the student's social isolation can be significant. Some students who have disabilities—even those supported by paraprofessionals—can undeniably have rich social lives, friendships, and social relationships. This chapter is intended to help improve the social lives of students such as Seth who are supported by paraprofessionals. Specifically, this chapter focuses on 1) the importance of friendships, 2) the Velcro phenomenon, 3) subtle and gentle supports, 4) natural supports, 5) your role as a bridge, 6) supporting unstructured time, 7) supporting structured time, 8) teaching the rules of social interaction, and 9) commonly asked questions.

THE IMPORTANCE OF FRIENDSHIPS

Think about your own life. How important are friendships? What do friends add to your life? For me, my own friends are critical to my quality of life. They provide entertainment; we have fun together; they act as a sounding board to help me deal with the trials of parenthood; and they share with me the joys and successes of life. My friends support me, and I, in turn, support them. I have always relied on my friendships—even when I was in school. When thinking about my own schooling experience, I most remember my motivation to get to school to see my friends. (Dare I say I was even more excited about seeing my friends than I was about the social studies lecture?) Similarly, friendships and relationships are a key part in every student's life.

"We humans want to be together. We only isolate ourselves when we are hurt by others, but alone is not our natural state" (Wheatley, 2002, p. 19). This chapter focuses on how paraprofessionals can facilitate students' relationships with their peers and bring people together instead of hindering the students' social interactions.

Think how it would be if someone were paid to be with you 8 hours a day, 5 days a week. How would your relationships change? Would you notice a loss of privacy, freedom, or intimacy? What do you think your friends and coworkers would think of this new addition into your life? Do you think they would avoid you? Do you think people would flock to you? Now, imagine . . . . How do you think your presence affects the students whom you support?

Sometimes, a paraprofessional is a magnet. Other students (particularly those in younger grades) want to connect with the adult and interact. But, the unintended consequence of paraprofessional support has been widely documented—specifically, the interference with peer relationships and friendships. Giangreco, Edelman, Luiselli, and MacFarland (1997) have identified several ways in which paraprofessional proximity (or the closeness of you to the student) can hinder students with disabilities. These include interference with the ownership (teachers see the student as "yours," not theirs) and responsibility of general educators, separation from classmates, dependence on adults, impact on peer interactions, limitations on receiving competent instruction, loss of personal control, loss of gender identity, and interference with the instruction of other students. Other studies have determined that the close proximity of a paraprofessional hinders the amount of peer interaction that occurs (Malmgren & Causton-Theoharis, 2006).

Embarrassment can be another factor. One student spoke of the embarrassment he felt at times over having a paraprofessional. He felt it was similar to having his mother with him:

> I was kind of getting embarrassed because I always had, like a mother right there. People were like looking at me and stuff, and saying, Why do you always have this person with you who is twice as old as you? (Broer, Doyle, & Giangreco, 2005, p. 420)

The placement of one student directly next to a paraprofessional (nearly attached) can be described as the *Velcro phenomenon.* As a paraprofessional, it is important to avoid being Velcroed to a student. Velcroing might include holding hands, walking next to a student, sitting next to a student, having a student on your lap, walking together in the halls, and so forth. There are many different alternatives to such intensive close proximity; I provide some suggestions in this chapter. See the sections "Five Ways to Naturally Support Students" and "Six Ways to Facilitate Relationships" in this chapter.

WHAT DOES RESEARCH SAY ABOUT VELCRO?

In a study I conducted with Kimber Malmgren, we observed a second-grade student named Gary as he worked in his classroom and played with his friends. Gary was supported by a paraprofessional throughout his day. During a 4-week period, Gary participated in only 32 interactions with his peers. Twenty-nine of those interactions occurred on the day when the paraprofessional was absent. Only three interactions occurred when the paraprofessional was with him, and the paraprofessional ended two of those three interactions by asking him to get back to work. Clearly, the presence of the paraprofessional had a significant impact on Gary's ability or willing-ness to connect with other students (Malmgren & Causton-Theoharis, 2006).

What do kids report about having paraprofessionals? Another important study examined the perspectives of high school students with disabilities attending general education classes with paraprofessional support. These students described their paraprofessionals' roles primarily in four ways: as 1) mother, 2) friend, 3) protector, and 4) primary teacher (Broer et al., 2005). The majority of the students in the study further "expressed powerful messages of disenfranchisement, embarrassment, loneli-ness, rejection, fear and stigmatization" (Broer et al., 2005, p. 427). These students can be powerful teachers to those responsible for their education. Paraprofessionals can learn from their voices and from those of other students to create supports that are not stigmatizing but that, instead, help students make friends and feel socially successful in school.

HIDING IN FULL VIEW: SUBTLE, GENTLE, AND RESPECTFUL SUPPORT

At this point in the book, I am moving to the "art" of paraprofessional support. Believe it or not, there is a great deal of finesse, subtlety, and elegance that goes into excellent paraprofessional support. This part of the job requires the most nuance, careful action, and, at times, inaction. As Jamie Burke, a high school student with autism, spoke about adult support and its impact on his social interactions, he emphasized that the support he received should be subtle so that it would not interfere with his desire for a social life. He stated, "We are willing and ready to con-nect with other kids, and adults must quietly step into the background, camouflag-ing their help as a tiger who may hide in full view" (Tashie, Shapiro-Barnard, & Rossetti, 2006, p. 185).

FIVE WAYS TO NATURALLY SUPPORT STUDENTS

Students need to move toward independence as they grow. Providing support in nat-ural ways is one way to help reduce dependence on support personnel. The following suggestions from Causton-Theoharis and Malmgren (2005) can help you maximize student independence and interdependence with peers and minimize student de-pendence on adults.

1. *Do not sit or place a chair meant for adult support next to a student.*

Where you position yourself during instruction is very important. There is rarely a rea-son to sit directly next to a student. Even if a student needs close support because of behavior or physical support, that student probably does not need you next to him or her 100% of the time. Never have a space permanently reserved for a paraprofessional next to a student. Remove the empty chair next to the student. Do not have any students sit on your lap or hold your hand unless that is commonly done for all students (e.g., in a preschool setting). If you feel that the expectation in a particular school or classroom is for you to sit next to a student, ask your team the following questions:

- When is it absolutely necessary to sit next to a student to provide one-to-one support? (Examples of this type of necessary support are when providing medical assistance or lifting/transferring a student.)
- Are there times during the day when I could provide the student with less support?
- If so, when?
- When and how can we help this student increase independence?
- When should I move away from this student?
- Could a peer provide key supports to this student?

2. *Do not remove the student.*

Friendships and relationships occur because of common experiences over long periods of time. Every time a student is removed from an inclusive classroom, that student loses potential time to interact, socialize, and learn with and from other students. If a student leaves for a sensory break, consider putting the sensory materials in the classroom; if a student is leaving because of challenging behavior, try to determine strategies that will help the student stay in the classroom (for strategies for working with students who have challenging behavior, see Chapter 8).

3. *Encourage peer support.*

If a student asks for your help with something, have the student ask a peer instead. Make this the norm for all students. One useful way to set this up is to have all students follow the rule, "Ask three before me." Set up partnerships during instructional time. Have students work together. Set up play partners, transition partners (partners for walking to and from classes), choice time partners, lunchtime partners, math partners, and so forth. Make sure the student you are supporting has a choice about whom he or she selects as a partner. Giving students the skills to seek peer support is a valid and important lifelong skill.

4. *Encourage independence and interdependence.*

If a student is able to complete a task in your presence without adult support, have him or her complete the task without supervision the next time. For example, Andrea had been having trouble getting her lunch tray to the lunch table, so the paraprofessional had been carrying it to the table for her. The paraprofessional soon realized that the issue was the weight of the tray and the drink. So, the paraprofessional took the drink off the tray, and Andrea was able to carry her tray to her table independently. Andrea then decided she would just take two trips (one with her tray and one with the beverage) without the paraprofessional helping.

Continually ask yourself what the next step is that will enable a student to become more independent and less dependent on adult support. If a student will still need assistance, consider having interdependence (or successfully completing the task with other students) be the goal. By the end of the year, sometimes Andrea's friend Will would carry her drink. Therefore, she would get to the table without any adult support and, instead, have the support of a friend.

5. *Fade your cues.*

One of the simplest, yet most effective ways to increase interaction for students is to fade the assistance of paraprofessionals. Fading assistance means actually reducing the type and level of support given to a student in a systematic way. Reducing support promotes independence, interdependence, and interaction with peers. Take a look at the cuing structure list shown in Table 6.1. The goal with this structure is always to

Table 6.1. Types of support

Type of support (listed from most intrusive to least)	Definition	Example
Full physical	Direct and physical assistance used to support a student	Hand-over-hand assistance while a student writes his or her name
Partial physical	Physical assistance provided for some of the total movement required for the activity	Put a zipper into the bottom portion and begin to pull up; the student then pulls the zipper up the rest of the way.
Modeling	A demonstration of what the student is to do	The paraprofessional does an art project; the student uses the art project as a model.
Direct verbal	Verbal information provided directly to the student	"Josh, stand up now."
Indirect verbal	A verbal reminder that prompts the student to attend to or think about what is expected	"Josh, what should happen next?"
Gestural	A physical movement to communicate or accentuate a cue (e.g., head nod, thumbs up, pointing)	Paraprofessional points to the agenda written on the board.
Natural	Providing no cue; allowing the ordinary cues that exist in the environment help the student know what to do	The bell rings for class. The teacher asks students to move to the rug. A message on the chalk board reads, "Turn to page 74."

Source: Doyle (2008).

move away from the most obtrusive (those on top) to the least obtrusive supports (those on the bottom) for students whenever possible (Doyle, 2008).

Providing natural or nonobtrusive supports is a very important first step toward helping students feel like everyone else. The next step in helping students connect with one another is to actually facilitate relationships and assist students with positive social interactions by becoming a bridge linking students and their peers.

YOUR ROLE AS A BRIDGE BETWEEN STUDENTS WITH DISABILITIES AND THEIR PEERS

You can become a bridge connecting students; you can blend in, provide more natural supports, and facilitate relationships among students. The following section offers six ways to help students relate to one another to form lasting friendships.

Six Ways to Facilitate Relationships

These ideas have been modified from Causton-Theoharis and Malmgren (2005):

1. *Highlight similarities among students.*

In a general education classroom, students are continually talking and sharing stories about things not related to the curriculum (e.g., hobbies, extracurricular activities). Become conscious of conversations going on around the student, and point out similarities. For example, as students are talking about T-ball, you might say, "Oh, Josh's sister plays T-ball." Or, as students are settling down with their library books, you might point out similarities among their books: "The two of you both selected books about computers. You can sit together and compare your books."

2. *Help students invite each other to socialize.*

Some students are very eager to socialize but do not know how to approach other students. It can be helpful for a paraprofessional to be proactive about all of the potential social situations that occur throughout the school day. Think ahead about social possibilities, and ask the student, "Who do you want to play with at recess today?" "How can you ask them?" "Who do you want to sit next to in study hall?" If you have a student who is nonverbal, provide a picture list of the students in the class and help the student program his or her device to ask a friend. An index card that says, "Do you want to play with me?" or "Will you be my partner?" can be very useful in such situations.

3. *Provide behavioral supports that are social in nature.*

When a student is rewarded for doing a good job, make the reception of the reward something social. This way, the reward can be more fun for all involved, and it will have the added benefit of allowing students to learn and practice social interaction. Some examples of these types of interactive behavioral supports follow:

- Have your student shoot baskets with a friend.
- Have your student eat lunch with a friend.
- Have your student make bead necklaces with a friend during study hall.
- Have your student play a computer game with a friend.
- Have your student go to the library and read with a friend.
- Have your student make an art project before school with a friend.

4. *Provide your student responsibilities that are interactive and collaborative.*

Students are commonly assigned responsibilities within the classroom and school environments. This is done to help students contribute to the classroom community and to build a sense of belonging. Paraprofessionals can be key participants in helping create partners for these tasks. For example, change the job chart in the classroom so that all jobs are done with buddies. When jobs arise in the classroom, ask students to do the jobs together: "Sue and Joryann, can you please pass out these papers?"

5. *Help other students understand.*

Peers are much more likely to interact with students if they understand necessary information about each other. Provide honest answers to students' questions. I once heard a little girl ask a paraprofessional, in reference to another student's FM device, "Why does he wear that thing on his head?" The paraprofessional said that it was private and that she should get back to work. The student got back to work, but an important question had been left unanswered. In the mind of the little girl, the subject was not to be talked about. As an unintended result, the student using the FM system might seem taboo. Your job is not to share confidential information about students with their peers, as was addressed in Chapter 4. However, there are times when providing basic information about a student or the type of support they are receiving may be helpful to the student. If you are unsure about whether to share information, ask the student and the special education service coordinator. As a more proactive way of addressing such subjects, some teaching teams have decided to bring their classes together to talk about what makes everyone special. For example, the students in one middle school classroom all listed things that made them unique. Then, they posted this information on a bulletin board. Some students included "I live with my grandmother" or "I speak two languages." One student in this class wrote, "I know sign language." This type of conversation can be used to describe specific behaviors or the accommodations that a student receives. Information can be shared about how and when to assist a particular student (e.g., do not talk in a baby voice, do ask whether he needs help). Before initiating a discussion of this type, make sure the student is comfortable with the plan, and involve both parties in deciding what information the student wants to share.

6. *Get out of the way!*

When a conversation among students has begun, give the students space so that a natural conversation can occur; eventually, a relationship may evolve. Think about where you should stand; try to be as unobtrusive to the student as possible. When I am teaching paraprofessionals to fade their support, a common mistake they make is to stand 3 or 4 feet away, keeping their eyes directly focused on the student. If you remain this close, it will be clear to everyone around that you are there, creating an invisible barrier between other students and the one you are supporting. Instead, while fading, move away and focus your attention on something else.

SUPPORTING UNSTRUCTURED TIME

Social interaction occurs at all times during the school day. Unstructured times are some of the most important times to provide support that will help students connect to one another. Examples of key times are listed in the following sections, with some suggestions that should be useful.

Before and After School

Students spend a lot of time traveling to and from school. This is a perfect time to facilitate social interaction. Before and after school, help the family find a travel partner or someone in the neighborhood to walk to school or ride the bus with the student.

In the Hallway

Have walking partners in the hallway between classes. A teacher with whom I once worked had the students go on "talk walks" as they traveled to and from class. Each student would receive an index card containing a quote from the book the class was reading, and the student would have to talk about the particular quote on his or her card. Or, the teacher would give each student a number and a partner, and the students would have to come up with as many mathematical equations that equal their numbers as possible. Another paraprofessional had a student push a student named Samantha in her wheelchair while another student walked alongside her. This allowed Samantha to have some space from an adult and a chance to converse. If a student does not use speech, program the device that the student uses to have common chatty phrases such as, "How's it going?" As the student moves through the hallway, he or she can start or initiate interactions.

At Lunchtime

Do not have students with disabilities sit together at one table. Instead, help students select lunch places at which they will feel the most comfortable and, at the same time, have increased likelihood of interacting with peers. Some schools create interest tables at which students' interests are printed on table tent cards (e.g., chess, Pokéman, rainforest animals). Students then sit at tables that interest them and can freely converse about their preferred topic. Other schools have "lunch bunches." Organizing a lunch bunch is a useful way to help a student who struggles with social interaction during the lunch period. A lunch bunch involves gathering a group of students to get together during the lunch period for a particular purpose (e.g., planning the end-of-year picnic, creating a class yearbook). This mixed group of students (not all students with disabilities) can meet weekly to complete the task. At the end of the year, the lunch bunch might celebrate the accomplishments with a pizza party. The objective is to bring students together in a more intimate setting, to foster social interaction and help form friendships. Music can be provided at lunchtime to create a calming atmosphere. A paraprofessional in one school employed this strategy because Jonah, the student with autism whom she supported, had found the lunchroom to be overloading to his senses. After asking him what kind of music he would like to have on, she piped Beatles music into the lunchroom, providing a calming atmosphere for all students. And, best of all, Jonah was able to stay in the lunchroom and connect with other students.

At Free or Choice Time

Help students choose the activities they want to do and which peers they want to participate. In high school, where a student sits is crucial. Have each student select his or her peers and location in a room by asking the student where he or she would prefer to sit, and respect that choice. During recess time, or during any other downtime outside of class, bring an activity that is particularly interesting to the student. For example, one of my students, Chelsea, loved to make beaded necklaces at home. So, the paraprofessional working with me brought a beading kit to class and told the students that they could use the kit as long as they shared it. She put it on Chelsea's desk and asked her to be responsible for it. When I walked out to recess to see how it was going, four girls and two boys had formed a semicircle around the bead kit, and all of them were making necklaces.

To Select Partners

As someone who has supported students in classrooms for a long time, the words I least like to hear are "Find a partner." Inevitably, as students clamor to work with their friends, someone will be left out and need a partner. If that happens, do not become the student's partner. Instead, help the student find a friend. It can be far more helpful to determine partners ahead of time. One very thoughtful paraprofessional, Corrie, tired of seeing the same scenario occur repeatedly during math class: One of

CLOCK BUDDIES

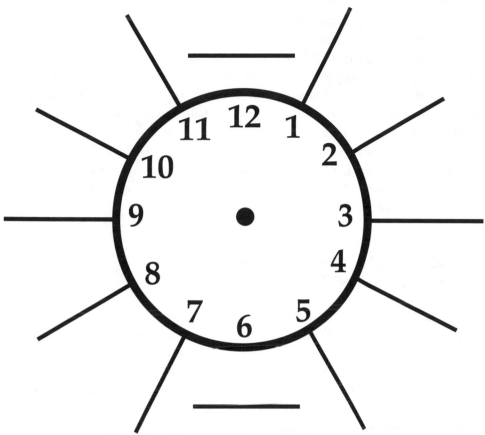

Figure 6.1. Clock Buddies sheet. (From Jones [1998–2006] Copyright © Raymond C. Jones. All Rights Reserved. http://www.ReadingQuest.org)

Corrie's students, Caleb, felt so bad every time partner selection occurred that he would not participate in the activity. Corrie worked with the math teacher to create partners who would remain constant so that this type of disruption would not have to occur. She found a Clock Buddies sheet online (see Figure 6.1) and, with the teacher's help, set up partners for the rest of the year by having students sign up on the Clock Buddies sheet. From that point on, when the teacher would say, "Find your 4:00 partner," Caleb knew exactly who his partner would be, and he was able to participate successfully in the math center.

SUPPORT DURING INSTRUCTIONAL TIME

During instructional time, walk around the room, supporting all students and answering everyone's questions. It can be very stigmatizing to be the only one receiving help. The best scenario is one in which you provide support to the entire class, with none of the students thinking that you are there to help a specific student. Avoid calling yourself "Claire's helper or assistant." Instead, refer to yourself as someone who supports everyone. As soon as a student has gotten started, do not hover. Give the student space to work and make mistakes, just like everyone else. Have the student request help in the same way that everyone else does. If you must redirect a student, do so quietly. Also praise quietly, and be careful not to nag. Each of these aspects is important, and your support should be as unobtrusive and gentle as possible.

To ensure that all students come into contact with a student with disabilities, you can move instructional materials to the student instead of asking the other students to go to a certain station or object. I witnessed a paraprofessional do this beautifully with Alex, a student in kindergarten who used a wheelchair. All of the students were moving over to a globe to gather information. The paraprofessional decided to move the globe over to Alex's desk, and, as the students came over to look at it, many of them interacted with Alex.

TEACH KIDS THE RULES OF SOCIAL INTERACTION

Many children or students struggle with *how* to interact with others. They feel they are playing a game in which they do not know the rules. If you are working with a child who feels this way, teach him or her the rules explicitly. But, do not teach the rules in isolation or in a separate room with only students who have disabilities. Instead, use everyday moments in the classroom and on the playground to artfully teach students how to interact with one another. There are many resources available to help you. Carol Gray has written several books on writing social stories for students with autism and on drawing social situations in cartoon form to help students understand social rules. Ask your team of teachers, or do some research online. Educators should not assume loneliness is part of the schooling experience; they can intervene and help students make and maintain friendships.

COMMONLY ASKED QUESTIONS ABOUT SOCIAL SUPPORTS

Q. This student's challenging behavior makes other kids not want to be around him or her. What do I do about that?

A. First, you have to assume that the student is worthy of friendships and relationships. Help support the student in a way that will both minimize the behavior and help others understand the behavior. One student, Kenny, used to rock back and forth when he felt anxious, and this behavior looked strange to Kenny's peers. Simply explaining to the other students what the behavior meant allowed one bright student to ask Kenny, "What can I do to help you stop rocking?" Kenny typed out a response: "Let me put my hand on your shoulder." From that moment on, Kenny's peers helped him to manage his rocking behavior, by asking, "Do you want to lean on me?"

Q. You suggest that I should not remove the learner, but one student has sensory issues that do not allow her to be in the lunchroom. What do I do about that?

A. Consider some of the lunchroom ideas discussed in this chapter. Make the lunchroom fit the student. Consider music, lunch partners, interest centers, or a quieter lunch space.

Q. I understand why I should fade my support, but I worry that people will think I am not doing my job. What can I do while I am fading my support?

A. This is a common concern. When moving away from a student, you can support other students, prepare for an upcoming class by creating modifications, take data on social interactions or behavior, read the student's individualized education program, help the teacher prepare for something upcoming, or search the school library and Internet for pictures and videos to support learning. You also can ask your team to brainstorm a list of ideas that fit your particular situation.

CONCLUSION

Seth was introduced at the beginning of this chapter. Seth is a student who struggles with social interactions. The biggest detriment to his social life is that he has an adult supporting him all school day long. Friendships and relationships are critical to Seth's development and quality of life. This is true for all students, and for those who are supported by a paraprofessional, care needs to be taken to ensure maximum social interaction. The suggestions mentioned in this chapter are meant to support your efforts to include students in the social aspects of school. The next chapter focuses on providing support during academic instructional time. But, be mindful that you often will need to provide both social and academic supports at the same time.

NOTES

7

Providing
Academic Supports

CLEARING A PATH
FOR PEOPLE WITH SPECIAL NEEDS
CLEARS THE PATH FOR EVERYONE!

I was surprised to find out that it doesn't take much to support Steven. By allowing him to draw his answer instead of writing it, he was able to represent the big ideas from the science lesson. Modifying can be surprisingly simple. It just takes some creativity and guidance from the special education teacher.

—Meghan (paraprofessional)

I personally use many different kinds of modifications throughout my own day. For example, I set my alarm to wake up. I go on a brisk walk before the demands of my day begin; this improves my ability to sit for long periods of time at work. I always set my keys in the same place in the kitchen so that I will not lose them and blame my husband or children for misplacing them. I use my electronic planner to keep my daily schedule. I always write my daily "to do" list on a large sticky note. I prioritize each item by writing numbers in the left-hand margin of the list. When I clean my house, I set my alarm for 15 minutes, and I race around the house to see how much I can get done before setting the alarm again for the next room. In meetings, I chew gum to keep myself attentive, and I sit close to the front so that I can keep myself from mentally wandering or chatting with my colleagues. My point is this: All people need their environments, time schedules, and behavior modified or adapted to allow them to be successful members of society. This chapter discusses some accommodations, modifications, and adaptations that are made for students with disabilities. I describe general and content-specific strategies and discuss the topic of assistive technology.

As a paraprofessional, you will provide modifications or adaptations to students and help them navigate the academic terrain of schooling. This can be a formidable task. The No Child Left Behind Act of 2001 (PL 107-110) also requires paraprofessionals to work with students "under the direct supervision of a certified staff member." The law stipulates that it is not the responsibility of paraprofessionals to decide the best modifications or adaptations to use with students. Instead, you should simply carry out written plans. Specifically, the regulations for paraprofessionals state that

> Paraprofessionals who provide instructional support must work under the direct supervision of a highly qualified teacher. (§§ 1119 [g][3][A]).
>
> A paraprofessional works under the direct supervision of a teacher if (1) the teacher prepares the lessons and plans the instructional support activities the paraprofessional carries out, and evaluates the achievement of the students with whom the paraprofessional is working, and (2) the paraprofessional works in close and frequent proximity with the teacher. (§ 200.59 [c][2] of the Title I regulations).

As a result, programs staffed entirely by paraprofessionals are not permitted. A certified teacher should write the lessons, and you should help students or review material. You should not be responsible for teaching new content. This chapter will familiarize you with several different types of modifications and specific ways to modify and adapt teachers' instructions to meet the needs of the students under your care. This chapter first describes general strategies that will enable you to support students, then discusses content-specific ideas, and, finally, suggests strategies that can help you work across all content areas. Consider reading this chapter with your teaching team.

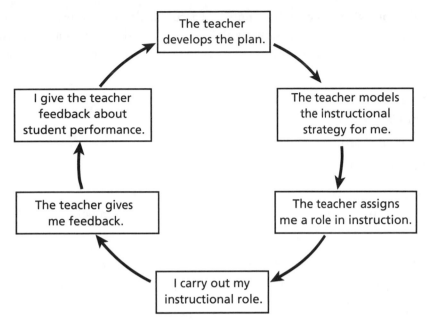

Figure 7.1. Cycle of support. (From Doyle, M.B. [2008]. *The paraprofessional's guide to the inclusive classroom: Working as a team* [3rd ed., p. 58]. Baltimore: Paul H. Brookes Publishing Co.; adapted by permission.)

Figure 7.1 shows a general cycle of support, which has been adapted from one developed by Mary Beth Doyle (2008).

ACCOMMODATIONS, MODIFICATIONS, AND ADAPTATIONS

The following information about the differences between modifications and adaptations comes from the PEAK Parent Center (n.d.) in Colorado Springs, Colorado. Accommodations and modifications are adaptations made to the environment, curriculum, instruction, or assessment practices that enable students with disabilities to be successful learners and to participate actively with other students in the general education classroom and in schoolwide activities.

Accommodations are changes in how a student accesses information and demonstrates learning. Accommodations do not substantially change the instructional level, content, or performance criteria. The changes are made to provide a student with equal access to learning and equal opportunity to show what he or she knows and can do. Accommodations can include changes in presentation, response format and procedures, instructional strategies, time and scheduling, environment, equipment, and architecture.

Modifications are changes in what a student is expected to learn. The changes are made to provide a student with opportunities to participate meaningfully and productively along with other students in classroom and school learning experiences. Modifications include changes in instructional level, content, and performance criteria.

The following lists contain examples of accommodations and modifications that can be provided in general education classrooms. Individualized education program teams determine accommodations and modifications that meet the unique and individual needs of their students.

Accommodations

- Test taken orally
- Large-print textbooks
- Additional time to take test
- A locker with an adapted lock
- Weekly home–school communication tool, such as a notebook or daily log book
- Peer support for note taking
- Lab sheets with highlighted instructions
- Graph paper to assist in organizing and lining up math problems
- Tape-recorded lectures
- Use of a computer for writing

Modifications

- An outline in place of an essay for a major project
- Picture Communication Symbol choices on tests
- Alternative books or materials on the same theme or topic
- Spelling support from a computerized spell-check program
- Word bank of choices for answers to test questions
- Use of a calculator on a math test
- Film or video supplements in place of text
- Questions reworded using simpler language
- Projects substituted for written reports
- Important words and phrases highlighted

Deciding which accommodations and/or modifications to use is a process that depends on the assignment and needs of each individual student. This process will be determined by a teacher, but a paraprofessional will have input on how these adaptations or modifications are carried out. When the appropriate adaptations are made, all students can have true access to the general education curriculum (PEAK Parent Center, n.d.).

GENERAL STRATEGIES

As soon as you assume they can't do something—the student won't be able to prove you wrong.

—Jay (paraprofessional)

Focus on Strengths

When providing support to students, it is easy to become overwhelmed by what they cannot do. For example, when I was providing support to Steven, a third grader with Down syndrome, it was easy to think, "Steven does not read; how am I to help him understand the science content in this chapter?" It helps to reframe your thinking and ask yourself what the student can do. Focus instead on the student's strengths; with Steven, you might think, "Steven is a very social guy. He can easily comprehend big ideas. He is masterful at drawing what he knows and labeling parts. He also can answer questions."

We focused on Steven's strengths of listening, social interaction, and understanding main ideas. When other students were required to quietly read the chapter from the science book, Steven's partner read the chapter aloud. At the end of each section in the text, Steven and his partner were required to say something about the section, and Steven, as he listened, worked on a drawing depicting the big ideas from that section. Steven and his partner then asked each other questions about the section and the drawing. This worked so well for Steven and his partner that the teacher decided to have the entire class read the science text that way for the rest of the year.

Ask the Student

If you are unsure about how to provide support, when to provide support, or how much support to provide, you do not need to make that decision alone. After discussing the student's support requirements with the general education and special education teachers, you should consult the student.

Keep Expectations High

Having a disability does not mean that a student cannot complete assignments and projects in the same way as anyone else. Before attempting to modify or alter a student's assignment, ask yourself whether the assignment actually needs any changes. Too often, education professionals overmodify for students or decide to make the same modification for every student with the same disability. Sometimes, the best thing to do for a student is not to change your expectations for him or her but, instead, to change the type or level of support.

Break Tasks into Smaller Steps

For some students, it might be useful to break tasks into smaller parts. For example, one student, Chelsea, preferred having a "to do" list posted on her desk for any independent work time. The paraprofessional would write down the big tasks that needed to be completed, and Chelsea would complete them independently and cross out each task. If you have a student who does not read, you could draw a picture list and have the student cross out each picture as he or she completes each task.

Extend Time on Tasks

Many students can complete the same work as anyone else if they have extra time. In these cases, it may be helpful to slowly decrease the time allotted for certain tasks. Or, if the other students have an hour to complete a test, allow the student to take the test in parts—one part on the first day, the second part on the next.

Present Limited Amount of Information on a Page

Some students prefer to see less information at once. The layout of information should be clean and free of distraction. Adequate white space, for example, can make an assignment appear less confusing. This modification can be made easily by copying different segments of an assignment onto different pages. In addition, white-out tape helps limit certain distracting information or pictures. Then, when you photocopy the item, the student has less information to wade through. An index card or a *word window,* a piece of cardboard with a small rectangular window with cellophane that allows students to see one line of text or one word at a time, can also help students eliminate information as they read by themselves.

Offer Support, Do Not Just Give It

Do not assume that a student needs help. If a student is struggling, encourage him or her to ask a peer first. If the student is still struggling, ask, "Can I help you get started?" If the student says, "No," respect his or her wishes.

Use a Soft Voice

Receiving support is not always a comfortable thing. It also can be distracting to classmates. Therefore, when students are working, use a soft voice.

Make Things Concrete

Many students need concrete examples, such as pictures or videos that support the concepts taught in class. Jill, a paraprofessional with whom I worked, would use down time to search the school library and Internet for pictures and videos to support learning.

The teacher would then incorporate these teaching aides into her mini-lectures and teaching centers. This not only helped the students with disabilities; everyone in the class benefited from these visual supports.

Teach Organizational Skills to Everyone

It is common for students with and without disabilities to struggle with organization. In one seventh-grade classroom, the paraprofessional helped everyone by doing binder checks at the end of each class. She made sure the notes were in the correct color-coded spot as students left the room. This helped not only Adam, who chronically struggled with keeping things organized, but countless others who needed similar support. Another paraprofessional made a checklist of all the items students needed to take home each day. These lists were made available for any student to use.

Change the Materials

Sometimes, all a student needs for success is a different type of material. A change in type, writing utensil, or size or type of paper can make a substantial difference for a student. For example, I used to work with a student named Brett. Every time Brett was expected to write, he would put his head down on the desk or angrily break pencils. The team of teachers and paraprofessionals who supported the classroom met and discussed the potential reasons for Brett's behavior and how they might make writing more pleasant for him. As a result of this conversation, the team decided to let all students choose their writing instruments and paper size. When this choice was offered, Brett chose a black, felt-tip marker and a half-sheet of paper. For some reason, the change of materials proved much better for him, and he wrote for longer periods of time. He later explained that he would get nervous if he saw "a whole blank piece of paper" and that he hated "the feel of the pencil on the paper."

Use a Timer

Izzy is a kindergarten student. Whenever transitions in the classroom occur, he has loud tantrums. Because of Izzy's difficulty with transitions, his team decides to use a timer to alert him when the transitions are coming. Izzy's teacher hands him an old track timer and tells him that he is in charge of letting the other students know when it is cleanup time. After first practicing with the timer, Izzy takes his responsibility very seriously. He walks around from group to group, reminding the kindergartners that there are only "5 minutes until cleanup time . . . 4 minutes . . . 3 . . . ." He continues to remind his friends until the timer goes off. He then shouts, "Clean up everyone!" For Izzy, the timer helps him know when the transition is occurring and also gives him an important responsibility. Timers can be useful for students who like to know how long tasks will take or who need help organizing their time. For some students, visual timers, or timers on which you can actually see how much time is left, can be particularly useful.

Preteach

Preteaching big ideas such as vocabulary or major concepts can be useful for many students. Preteaching should be done before a concept is "officially" taught to the rest of the class. You may introduce a concept, term, or idea to a student before the rest of the students learn it. For example, as the students were preparing for a magnet lab, Mr. Marco taught some of the key science vocabulary to Brett before the lesson. Brett entered the magnet lab understanding the terms *attract* and *repel.* This allowed Brett to come into the class prepared and more confident.

Peer Support

Peer support is one of the best ways to support students. Have all the students work in teams or partnerships. Tell students that their job is to help each other. However, some caution is necessary regarding peer support. Do not set up "helping relation-ships"—for example, Sonja always helps Jose. Instead, encourage students to help each other. Figure out times when Jose can help Sonja and others in the classroom.

Use Movement

Most students need to move often. When memorizing discrete concepts or pieces of information, use visual cues, signs, or movements. Many students who have trouble memorizing can use movements or visual cues. Challenge students to come up with their own movements that match the concepts of specific words. As an example, one sixth-grade teacher did spelling aerobics. When spelling words, if the letters were "tall letters" (e.g., *t, l, b*), the students would stand up tall and put their arms up; if letters were "short" (e.g., *o, e, a*), the students would put their hands on their hips; and, if letters hung below the line (e.g., *p, g, q*), the students would touch their toes. For instance, to spell the word *stop,* the students would touch their waists, reach up, touch their waists, and then touch their toes. What makes this particular example so pow-erful is that the movement is purposeful and connected to the content.

CONTENT-SPECIFIC STRATEGIES

What follows is a list of different modifications and adaptations of ways to approach different types of content and activities that are commonly used across content areas.

Remember, you will not be responsible for coming up with these ideas; that is the teacher's job. But, you should know these types of modifications and how best to use them with students. If you see an idea in Table 7.1 that you would like to try with a student, talk to the team to decide whether it would be an effective strategy. Discuss how to use it, when to use it, and when you might fade the strategy or idea.

Table 7.1. Content-specific modifications

In this subject	Consider these modifications, adaptations, and accommodations
Reading/language arts	Listen to books on tape/CD.
	Read with a peer.
	Follow along with a word window.
	Read from a computer with headphones.
	Work with a peer and have him or her summarize.
	Read enlarged print.
	Use CCTV (closed circuit TV)—a video magnifier that enlarges the font.
	Rewrite stories in more simple language.
	Use books with repetitive texts.
Mathematics	Calculators
	Touch math (each number has the correct number of dots on the actual number)
	Hundreds charts
	Number lines
	Flash cards
	Count stickers
	Manipulatives (e.g., unifex cubes, counting chips)
	Worksheet modified with easier-to-read numbers
	Pictures or visuals
	Larger cubes
	Chart paper to keep track of columns
	Talking calculator
	Numbered dice instead of dotted dice
	Real-world problems—problems with students' names in them

(Continued)

Table 7.1. *(Continued)*

In this subject	Consider these modifications, adaptations, and accommodations
Physical education	Different-sized sporting equipment
	Silent activities (for those who are sensitive to noise)
	Choice stations
	Change the size of the court
Art	Choice of materials
	Bigger/smaller materials
	Slant board
	Precut materials
	Stencils
	Smocks and aprons with pockets
	Gloves for kids who don't like to get messy
	Wiki sticks
	Posted steps about the process
	Modified scissors
Science	Hands-on experiences
	Teacher demonstration
	A role play
	Guest speaker
	Posted steps indicating the process
Social studies	Highlighters or highlighting tape
	A way to connect the content to self
	DVDs
	Visuals
	Maps
	A written task card (a card with a step-by-step process on it)
Music	Songs in the student's native language
	Instruments
	Signs while singing
	Rhythms to clap out
	Tapes/CDs of music to practice at home
	Music videos to watch

Literacy Support

Causton-Theoharis, Giangreco, Doyle, and Vadasy (2007) have determined at least five elements associated with the successful use of paraprofessionals to improve student outcomes.

1. The paraprofessional provides supplementary instruction (not primary instruction).

2. Instruction is designed in a way that does not require significant instructional decision making by the paraprofessional.

3. Proven instructional methods are used.

4. Paraprofessionals are trained in the instructional approach that they are expected to implement.

5. Paraprofessionals are supervised and monitored to ensure consistency of instruction.

If any of these conditions for providing content-specific instruction are not present, talk with your team to discuss how these elements could be implemented.

Commonly Occurring Activities Across Content Areas

Support can look very different for students in different content areas. Sometimes, a different teacher is responsible for each content area, and this can result in different expectations. Some students prefer certain subjects and perform better in them. For example, Ricky enjoyed music, so he needed almost no support in that class. He would enter the music room, gather his folder and instrument, and be ready to go. In science, he did not seem fond of the teacher or the subject, and he therefore needed more support to get started with tasks. Although a student's support might look different from class to class, teachers use similar activities across different subject areas. Table 7.2 highlights activities that are used commonly across subjects. Teachers may require students to do any number of these things throughout the day. Nonetheless, different students may have difficulty with each of these activities, for different reasons. The considerations listed on the right side of Table 7.2 have proven helpful for many students of all abilities.

Table 7.2. Common activities and supports

When the students are asked to . . .	Consider providing students . . .
Sit and listen	Visuals to look at
	Movement breaks
	An FM system (that amplifies the teacher's voice)
	A rug or mat to help determine where to be
	An object to signify who is speaking (e.g., a talking stick)

(Continued)

Table 7.2. *(Continued)*

When the students are asked to . . .	Consider providing students . . .
	A ball to sit on
	Choice about where to sit
	A focus object for students to hold or manipulate
	A signal to start listening
	The book that is being read
	A topic bag—filled with objects that relate to the content
	A job to do (help another student, write ideas on the board)
Present orally	Choice about the supports necessary
	Note cards
	Visuals
	A handout
	A voice recorder
	A videotape/DVD
	A microphone
	PowerPoint
	Preprogrammed communication device
Take a test	A review of test strategies
	A review of the information
	A practice test
	A double-spaced test
	Easy questions first
	A reader for the test
	A reduced number of choices by eliminating one or two choices
	In matching, divided a long column into smaller section
	A computer
	As much time as needed
	An oral exam
	A performance-based test
	The option of drawing or labeling
	Simplified language

Complete worksheets	A word bank
	Clear directions
	File folder labels for students to stick answers onto
	Highlighted directions
	Fewer problems or questions
	Choice about type of writing instrument
Discuss	A talking object
	Note cards with students' ideas written on them
	Peer support
	A preprogrammed communication device with a question on it
	A piece of paper to draw ideas or concepts
	Choice about how to participate in the discussion
	The text the students are discussing
	A highlighted section of the text—have the student read and others discuss
Take notes	A lecture outline to complete during the lecture
	A chart
	A graphic organizer
	The teacher's notes from the day before
	An AlphaSmart
	Choice about how to take notes
	A copy of the teacher's notes with key words eliminated
	Lecture notes with pictures
	Photocopies or carbon copies from another student
	A laptop computer
Use a computer	A task card for how to start up the program
	Modified keyboard
	Enlarged font
	Intellikeys
	An adjusted delay on the mouse
	An alphabetical keyboard
	Large keyboard
	Choice about what to work on

(Continued)

Table 7.2. *(Continued)*

When the students are asked to . . .	Consider providing students . . .
Read a text	Book on tape
	Larger print font
	Highlighter
	Choral reading
	Background information about the text
	Bullets of the main ideas
	Sticky notes to write questions on
	"Just-right books"
	Puppets
	Reading light
	Choice about what to read
Be organized	Color-coded folders
	A planner
	An agenda written on the board
	Assignments written on the board in the same place
	Assignments that are already three-hole punched
	A picture schedule
	A sticky note on desk of things to do
	A homework folder
	A desk check
	Clock or timer on desk
	A verbal rehearsal of the schedule
	A consistent routine
Write	Tell a friend your story before writing it
	Discuss as a whole group
	Use graphic organizers
	Use bullet writing
	Use pencil grips
	Student dictates the story to you or a peer.
	Teacher writes words on a separate piece of paper student rewrites

Use stickers to fill in blanks

Draw instead of write

Use raised-line paper—so students can feel lines

ASSISTIVE TECHNOLOGY

Assistive technology is any type of technology that helps people with disabilities perform functions that might otherwise be difficult or impossible. The official definitions of *assistive technology* are as follows:

> Assistive technology in special education refers to any devices or services that are necessary for a child to benefit from special education or related services or to enable the child to be educated in the least restrictive environment. (IDEA 2004, 34 C.F.R. §300.308)

> The term *assistive technology device* as outlined in IDEA 2004 means any item, piece of equipment, or product system, whether acquired commercially off the shelf, modified, or customized, that is used to increase, maintain or improve functional capabilities of children with disabilities. (20 U.S.C. § 1401 [a][25])

> The term *assistive technology service* means any service that directly assists a child with disabilities in the selection, acquisition, or use of an assistive technology device. The term includes:

> • The evaluation of the needs of a child with a disability, including a functional evaluation of the child in the child's customary environment;

> • Purchasing, leasing, or otherwise providing for the acquisition of assistive technology devices by children with disabilities;

> • Selecting, designing, fitting, customizing, adapting, applying, maintaining, repairing, or replacing of assistive technology devices;

> • Coordinating and using other therapies, interventions, or services with assistive technology devices, such as those associated with existing education and rehabilitation plans and programs;

> • Training or technical assistance for a child with disabilities or, where appropriate, the family of a child with disabilities;

> • Training or technical assistance for professionals (including individuals providing education or rehabilitation services), employers, or other individuals who provide services to, employ, or are otherwise substantially involved in the major life functions of individuals with disabilities. (20 U.S.C. § 1401 [a][26])

Assistive technology includes mobility devices (e.g., walkers or wheelchairs), software, keyboards with large keys, software enabling students who are blind to use computers, or text telephones that enable students who are deaf to talk on telephones. A student who struggles with the fine motor skills involved with writing might use an AlphaSmart device, and a student who struggles to communicate might type his or her ideas into a computer, which then speaks the ideas aloud. If a student uses one type of assistive technology or another, you should learn as much as you can about the technology. If possible, ask for specific training on the technology so that you can assist the student in using the device, programming it, or fixing it if necessary. See the appendix (p. 93) for a list of useful web sites and resources for assistive technology.

TWENTY-ONE WAYS TO USE A STICKY NOTE

I once knew a paraprofessional who wrote the student she supported a positive note on a sticky note every day. The student brought that note home and read it with his parents. The purpose of these notes was to provide only positive comments to the student. These kind notes really helped the student feel good about his performance at school. Sticky notes are amazingly versatile. When I give presentations to teachers, I often challenge them to think of as many ways as they can to use sticky notes to support students academically. Figure 7.2 shows 21 great ideas.

COMMONLY ASKED QUESTIONS ABOUT ACADEMIC SUPPORT

Q. One student asks me to "go away" when I work with him. I cannot just let him sit there and fail. What should I do?

A. Listen to the student. If a student requests that you not work with him or her, do not support the student at that time. Instead, figure out how you might provide support without being physically next to the student. The lists in this chapter should be helpful to you.

Q. When a direction is given, a student just calls my name and asks me to come and help. I am trying to fade my support, but the student will not do anything without me by her side. What should I do?

A. This student has become very dependent on adult support. I would suggest talking to the student about the need to try things by herself or about asking peers for help. Encourage all students in the class to use and provide help to one another. Involve your team in determining ways to increase the student's independence. Make sure the solutions will make the student feel empowered to become more independent—not punished for her dependence.

Q. I am really just left to figure out how to support my students. What should I do if I receive almost no direction from a teacher?

A. This is a common and major problem. You should first set aside time with the teacher who is directing your work. Be prepared with a list of questions. Ask for the support you need to do your job. Here are some questions to get you started:

- Could I have a written plan to follow throughout my day?

21 Ways to
Use a Sticky Note

- As an individual agenda

- As a to-do list

- For a positive note in a pocket

- To mark page numbers

- As a reading guide

- To highlight sections of text

- To place under the directions

- To write questions to the students in their reading books

- As a written reminder about behavior

- As a way to monitor hand raising (every time they raise their hand and answer, they mark the note)

- To cover up sections of a worksheet

- As a word bank (so students don't have to write but can, instead, place word in blank)

- For students who have a lot to say and blurt out a lot—have them write their questions on sticky notes and select one or two to ask

- To add ideas to a brainstormed list

- For students to give feedback to each other on projects or papers

- To label parts of a diagram

- To create a matching game

- To put students into groups

- For students to write questions or comments and then to give to their teacher as a ticket out the door

- To ask a question to a peer, such as "Do you want to sit with me at lunch?"

- To summarize the main idea of a lesson, story, or activity

Figure 7.2.   Twenty-one ways to use a sticky note.

- Could you please tell me specifically what to do when the student gets anxious, gets out of his desk, or [fill in a concerning behavior here]?

- When I support the students in math, could you give me an outline telling me what to do?

When you meet with the teacher, be specific and ask your questions directly. If you still do not get the answers you need to effectively support the student, consider going to someone else (e.g., the principal, the director of special education, or anyone else with whom you feel comfortable talking) and letting them know you need more support. The bottom line is that you are required by law to receive support and supervision by a certified teacher.

CONCLUSION

As a paraprofessional, you will not decide which modifications, adaptations, assistive technology, or data collection procedures are used. Nevertheless, it is very helpful to become familiar with the multitude of ways students can be supported. Careful support is critical when providing support to students during academic work time. The time that a teaching team spends discussing the types of support necessary to enable students to learn certain subjects or perform certain activities, how to fade support, and how to best adapt material and instruction across curricular areas is time well spent. Interestingly, when teams make these changes for specific students, they can end up making improvements to teaching for all students. See the cartoon (at the beginning of the chapter) for an illustration of this concept. This chapter has focused on the many ways you can use strategies to support academics. The next chapter highlights behavioral support strategies.

Chapter 7 Appendix

Useful Web Sites and Resources for Assistive Technology

CAST: Transforming Education through Universal Design for Learning
http://www.cast.org

National Center to Improve Practice in Special Education Through Technology, Media and Materials
http://www2.edc.org/NCIP

ACCESS IT: The National Center on Accessible Information Technology in Education
http://www.washington.edu/accessit/index.html

NATRI: National Assistive Technology Research Institute
http://natri.uky.edu

ABLEDATA: Your source for assistive technology information
http://www.abledata.com

CATEA: National public website on assistive technology
http://www.assistivetech.net

The Alliance for Technology Access: Connecting children & adults with disabilities to technology tools
http://www.ataccess.org

University of Connecticut Center for Students with Disabilities
http://www.csd.uconn.edu/handbook_5d.html

Rehabtool.com: World-class Assistive Technology
http://www.rehabtool.com/at.html

NOTES

8

Providing Behavioral Supports

CONSIDERING HER STUDENTS WITHOUT
DISABILITIES, MRS. BAKER
REALIZES DAVID'S UNUSUAL
BEHAVIORS AREN'T THAT UNUSUAL.

I haven't had enough training to handle this kid. If I tell him to stop, he continues. If I try to make him stop, he screams. I literally don't know what to do when he is out of control.

—Ben (paraprofessional)

I recently learned that at school they were restraining my child. They were actually lying on top of him. It made me sick to think about how powerless he must have felt. I marched in the next day, and that situation has changed . . . . But I think about that every day.

—Tracy (parent)

I once was giving a presentation to a large group of teachers. I asked them to list the most challenging behaviors they had seen among their students. The teachers thought about it for a while and then shared their lists with me as I wrote their ideas on chart paper. The lists included swearing, fighting, yelling, shutting down, becoming silent, running out of the room, hitting, and injuring oneself (e.g., biting one's own arm).

I then asked this same group of teachers whether they ever had participated in those behaviors themselves. I told them to raise their hands if they ever had sworn, fought, yelled, shut down, become silent, run out of a room, hit someone, or done anything to hurt themselves. The sound of nervous laughter filled the room as almost everyone raised their hands. This is no reflection about that particular group of teachers. Most people behave in ways that would be considered challenging or concerning. When I then asked the teachers to distinguish the students' challenging behaviors from their own behavior, one teacher responded, in a half-joking manner, "When I have bad behavior, I have a darn good reason!" Guess what? So do students.

I next asked the group to think about what they needed when they had bad behavior. They brainstormed this list: a hug, time away, someone to listen, a glass of wine, a nap, a cool-off period, changing the subject, talking to someone. I personally consider this a good list. Many of those things also help me calm down when I am angry or upset. Notice, however, not only what they suggested, but also what was *not* suggested. No teacher reported needing a sticker chart. No one said they needed to be lectured or be kicked out of the room. Instead, like most people, these adults needed support, comfort, and calm, gentle understanding. Guess what? Students need that, too.

In your job, you likely will work with students who have challenging behaviors. These may range from relatively nonconfrontational behaviors such as skipping class or shutting down to more significant or externalizing behaviors such as fighting with other classmates, running out of the school, or hurting oneself. This chapter begins with a discussion of typical responses to challenging behaviors and an overview of positive behavioral supports. Then, I present a series of recommendations of what to do before, during, and after students demonstrate these types of challenging behaviors. At the end of the chapter, I answer some commonly asked questions.

THE TYPICAL RESPONSE TO CHALLENGING BEHAVIOR

Herb Lovett (1996), a researcher who was at the Institute of Disability at the University of New Hampshire, described the typical response to challenging behavior:

> Our initial response to an unwanted behavior, is to react, to correct what we perceive to be unacceptable, inappropriate behavior. The thinking behind this perception is that the person exhibiting the behavior has lost control and that those who are in charge—in control—are responsible for regaining it through the application of methods and technologies specifically designed for this purpose. (p. 136)

The major problem with this type of response is that when the chosen method of control does not work, the teacher or paraprofessional tends to become frustrated and, consequently, use more punitive methods for control. The intentions backfire, and, through a need to control and correct, teachers and paraprofessionals often create formidable barriers that further alienate them from those they are supposed to support and teach (Lovett, 1996). What follow are ideas and suggestions to move away from these typical responses to behavior toward a much more humanistic method of supporting students.

POSITIVE BEHAVIORAL SUPPORT

> *Positive behavioral supports* have been developed as a movement away from the traditional mechanistic, and even aversive behavior management practices that were being applied to students with disabilities. This approach emphasizes the use of collaborative teaming and problem solving processes to create support that stress prevention and remediation of problem behaviors through the provision of effective educational programming and the creation of a supportive environment. (Janney & Snell, 2008, p. 2)

The basic tenets of positive behavioral supports are as follow:

1. Behavior is learned and can change.

2. Intervention is based on studying the behavior.

3. The intervention emphasizes prevention and teaching new behaviors.

4. Outcomes are personally and socially valued.

5. Intervention requires comprehensive, integrated supports. (Carr et al., 2002; Janney & Snell, 2008)

Note that positive behavioral supports require a team approach. You should not be expected to design a positive behavioral support program. Nevertheless, understanding the basic tenets of the program is important because you likely will be responsible for helping to carry out behavioral plans for some students.

PROACTIVE BEHAVIORAL MANAGEMENT

Most challenging behavior can be avoided or managed by thinking ahead. Thinking ahead involves determining what works for the student.

....

Gabe, a student with autism, has a very difficult time with changes in his schedule. He needs to know when transitions will occur. If he is surprised by a change in the schedule, he hides in his locker, paces, or runs around the room. One way to avoid this issue is to prepare Gabe for each day's schedule. The teaching team does this by having a peer greet Gabe's bus in the morning. Gabe and his peer then walk to the room together, and when they reach the classroom, they review the agenda for the day. Gabe also has an individual copy of the schedule in his planner. This strategy represents one of the most successful ways to prepare Gabe for the day ahead and to reduce his anxiety about the schedule.

....

Building a Relationship

Herb Lovett (1996) has highlighted the importance of relationships and connections as more central than anything else related to supporting students behaviorally:

> A positive approach [to behavior] invites people to enter into the same sort of relationship that most of us have and treasure: ongoing, with mutual affection and regard. In such relationships, we all make mistakes, are all in some ways inadequate and yet it is not the level of success that is the ongoing commitment. In the context of relationships, the success and failure of our work becomes harder to assess because the key elements no longer involve simply quantity but the more complex issues of quality. We professionals have routinely overlooked the significance of relationships. (p. 137)

Getting to know your students and learning what they enjoy can be a truly helpful way to address challenging behaviors. "Creating a suitable level of rapport with students is an absolute essential prerequisite for helping students behave" (Knoster, 2008, p. 25).

....

Lisa, a paraprofessional working with Connie, a high school student with Down syndrome, was having a difficult time getting to know Connie. They just were not clicking. Lisa decided to go to Connie's house on the weekend to get to know her better.

Lisa asked her teammates and Connie's parents for their consent. Connie showed Lisa all around her house and introduced her to her brother and grandmother. Most important, Lisa met Connie's dog, Champ. Lisa indicated that this home visit was one of the most important ways to break down Connie's walls and for them to begin to trust one another. When Connie was interviewed about her relationship with Lisa, Connie said, "I trust her. We get through the good and bad times together. Without that, I do not know what I would do."

············

Clearly, Lisa created an opportunity for Connie to trust her. She achieved this through a home visit and by continuing to be a trustworthy figure in Connie's life. But, there are many different ways to form relationships and to let students know that you trust them and that they can trust you. Some different methods include generally being there for the student if he or she needs you, having fun with the student, learning about the student's home life without making a home visit, seeing the same movies that the student enjoys, participating in the same activities the student likes, and talking to the student about his or her friends and hobbies. The next section discusses additional ways to build rapport each day with students.

How Do I Build Rapport with Students?

Latham (1999) provides steps for parents to build rapport with their children. These steps have been modified for paraprofessional use with students and are included here:

1. Demonstrate age-appropriate touch (high-five, hand shake), facial expressions (reflect the nature of the situation), tone of voice (e.g., your voice also should match the situation), and body language (e.g., appear relaxed, keep your arms open, be attentive, look at the student).

2. Ask open-ended questions (e.g., "What are you doing after school?" "What was your favorite part of the movie?").

3. Listen while the student is speaking. Ideally, talk less than the student (do not interrupt or change the subject).

4. Demonstrate the use of empathetic statements. Act like a mirror and reflect the child's feelings by expressing your understanding and caring.

5. Ignore nuisance behavior and let the little stuff slide.

Matching Instructional Practices to Student Strengths

One of the most simple ways to support students' positive behavior is to match instructional techniques to student strengths. For example, when a student who is a successful artist is allowed to draw his or her ideas during the social studies lecture, the student is more likely to be engaged and have positive behavior. As a paraprofessional, you will not have a lot of control regarding how the instruction is planned. However, some paraprofessionals have very successfully helped teachers integrate new instructional techniques that support student learning. By trying out ideas and putting new plans in place, you can discover alternative approaches that others on the team also can try. You can always suggest new ideas. Never underestimate your power and creativity in supporting the students with whom you work.

··········

Sue (a paraprofessional) supports a student (Alex) who needs to move often. Sue asks the general education teacher whether they can put chart paper on the wall and have all students stand and use markers to do a brainstorming activity instead of doing it at their desks. The teacher is willing to try it. Alex is more successful, and the other students seem to really enjoy this approach.

Before this, Alex was considered naughty because he never sat still. He was always out of his seat, wiggling and moving. What Sue sensed was that Alex's misbehavior indicated a learning preference (a bodily kinesthetic learning preference). Sue had an idea for putting more movement into Alex's learning.

··········

Knowing and understanding how students misbehave can help you identify what they need. Research has demonstrated that taking advantage of students' strengths has been shown to decrease negative behavior and increase on-task behaviors (Kornhaber, Fierros, & Veenema, 2004). See the following examples:

- If students are constantly moving or are bodily kinesthetic learners, they need more movement during instruction. For example, EunYoung needs to move during instruction. So, when the teacher reads aloud to the class, EunYoung is allowed to sit in a rocking chair. The teachers in EunYoung's class let the students sit however they like during certain class activities.

- If students are continually talking or are interpersonal learners, they need more interaction during learning. For example, Gwen works best when she is able to talk with peers. So, before writing a journal entry, she is given a few minutes to talk to a friend about what she plans to write.

- If students are constantly singing or are musically gifted, they need more music in school. Lucy enjoys music, so the teacher uses music during writing workshops. The music helps Lucy stay focused, and other students also enjoy it.

- If students enjoy making connections to their own lives or are intrapersonal learners, they need more time during school to make personal connections to the content. For example, Jerry enjoys making personal connections. So, during the *Little House on the Prairie* unit, Jerry's assignment is to determine how each of the settlers is like him and different from him.

- If students draw or doodle or are spatial learners, you can make art part of the learning process. For example, Rubin likes to draw. So, while he listens to a mini-lecture about cellular division, Rubin has the option of drawing the concepts.

- If a student enjoys mathematical calculations or is highly logical, you can use math and logic to strengthen student's learning in other subjects. For example, Jorge loves math and struggles during English. So, the paraprofessional has Jorge make Venn diagrams, time lines, and graphs about the characters in *Romeo and Juliet*. This helps him keep track of all of the characters, and, during discussion, he shares his charts with other students to help them remember the details of the book.

Set Up the Environment in a Way That Promotes Positive Behavior

Have you ever walked into a classroom that felt controlled and stiff? Have you ever been in a learning environment that you wanted to escape from? What type of learning environment promotes learning? The following list offers ideas to help promote a more comfortable classroom environment.

- Arrange desks in a way that allows for easy student interaction. A circle of desks grouped into tables is more likely to promote interaction.

- Seat students with disabilities in different locations in the room. Do not group students with disabilities together.

- Create a calm, relaxed place in which students feel comfortable moving around and engaging with others.

- Create structure by posting the agenda or daily schedule.

- Do not isolate any student by seating him or her in a separate location.

- Make it feel like a space for students by adorning the walls with student work.

- Have music playing softly in the background at times.

- If students are expected to sit on the floor, a soft, carpeted place will make them feel more comfortable.

- If a student struggles with personal space, have all students sit on carpet squares.

- If a student does not like to be called on in class without warning, set up a system to let the student know when the teacher will call on him or her.

Although paraprofessionals are often deployed after challenging behaviors have started, a better use of paraprofessional time and energy is in helping create comfortable and relaxed environments so that problematic behaviors are less likely.

Meet Students' Needs

All human beings require certain things to be happy and, therefore, well behaved. These things have been called *universal desires* (Lovett, 1996). Autonomy, relationships, interdependence, safety, trust, self-esteem, belonging, self-regulation, accomplishment, communication, pleasure, and joy are needs for all human beings. Helping students meet these needs is essential to creating learning environments in which students feel comfortable and safe; such feelings, in turn, help resolve behavioral issues.

Autonomy   *Autonomy* means the right or power to govern oneself or to be self-determined. To help students feel autonomous, provide choices and allow them to make as many decisions as possible. Examples include choice in location of seat, whom to sit by, the materials to use for a project, the topic of a project, the type of writing instrument, whether to have something modified, and what to eat. Allowing students more choices enhances their ability to make decisions and become independent people.

Relationships and Interdependence   An entire chapter of this book has been dedicated to relationships. This is because relationships are deeply important. Students need to be allowed to have relationships and connections with their peers. Opportunities should be created for students to help one another. Chapter 6 suggests several strategies for facilitating relationships and building connections among students. When these needs are not met, students will invariably try to gain each other's attention. This occurs in a variety of ways: it may be through hitting, tapping, or pestering. Students might also seem lonely and choose to sit by themselves. They may seem angry and try to get removed from certain settings through challenging behaviors.

Safety and Trust   Creating a safe, trusting relationship requires you to follow through when you say you are going to do something. Demonstrate that you can be trusted and that you are not there to punish or hurt any students. Keep your promises to students. "Many people who engage in difficult behaviors have too much experience with broken promises" (Pitonyak, 2007, p. 18). Continually send the message that you are there to be trusted to help and support, not to punish and manage. Do not remove students from the learning environment. Every time a student is removed for a time-out or a brief stint in the hall, a clear message is sent to that student. The message is, "You are not welcome here. Your membership in this community is contingent on your behavior." This tends to create a vicious cycle: Students feel that they do not belong, and they act in ways to demonstrate such feelings; if they are removed, their suspicions are reinforced.

Pleasure and Joy   All students need pleasure and joy in their learning environments. When supporting a student, ask yourself, "How often does this student experience pleasure or joy in the classroom?" "How often does this student laugh or have fun with others?" "How can more time be devoted to pleasure and joy in the environment?"

Communication   All students deserve the right to communicate their needs and wants. Once, when I was observing students in a classroom, the teacher asked about the weather and date. One student using a communication device pushed a button to make the device say, "I know the answer." He pushed the button again and pushed it three more times during the morning meeting. He was never called on to answer. It seemed that the teacher was beginning to feel frustrated by the noise of the device, and she eventually walked over and took the device away from him. He later found the device and pushed the button to make the device say, "I feel sad." This story illustrates an important point. Communication is not something to be earned and taken away. Any attempt to communicate should be honored because all people need to be heard.

If students do not feel as if they are being heard, they will attempt to communicate their thoughts, feelings, and needs through their behavior. Students will assert their own independence, behave in certain ways to receive pleasure and joy, act out when they do not feel safe or need to communicate something, and simply act out to create more pleasure and joy in their lives. Purposefully creating such opportunities is essential to helping students avoid negative behavior. Students might be communicating something such as, "I am lonely," "I do not feel safe," or "I do not know how to tell you what I need." The behavior they exhibit might not be easy to identify as communication, but it is important to remember that all behavior is communication. Part of the job of educators is trying to figure out what students are attempting to communicate in their behavior.

Ask Yourself: What Does This Person Need?

For each student, make a plan to help him or her receive more of the things that will fulfill his or her needs. For example, if you believe a student needs more choice, you should provide the student more choice.

I am aware that this recommendation contradicts most behavior systems and plans. Many people believe that if you give others what they need, they will just act out more. The opposite, however, is true. If you help meet students' needs, they will not need to behave more to get what they want (Kluth, 2003; Lovett, 1996; Pitonyak, 2007).

Here are some great questions to ask yourself:

- What might this person need?
- Does this person need more pleasure and joy in his or her school day?
- Does this person need more choice or control over what happens to him or her?
- Does this person need to feel more as if he or she belongs?
- Does this person need more relationships and interdependence?
- Does this person need more autonomy?
- Does this person need more access to communication?

First, determine each student's needs, and then work with your team to determine avenues to meet those needs.

WEATHERING THE STORM

When confronting challenging behavior, school personnel often react by imposing consequences, threatening to impose consequences, removing rewards, or ignoring the behavior; in some instances, school personnel might force students to behave. Forcing a student to behave might involve physically moving a student or providing hand-over-hand assistance.

I remember watching one student having difficult behavior in a classroom. The student was supposed to be working with the occupational therapist with some unifix cubes. Instead, the student began running and throwing the cubes at the occupational therapist. The therapist responded by saying, "If you do not stop, I will write your name on the board, and you will lose recess time." The student did not stop. The occupational therapist walked over and wrote the student's name on the board in large letters. The student became loud and continued running around. The therapist then put a checkmark next to the student's name as more unifix cubes rained down on her head. She eventually said, "You are going to the time-out room!" She brought the student kicking and screaming to the time-out room, where he spent 2 hours, screaming, until he eventually fell asleep.

These types of situations are very difficult; you may have witnessed similar situations before. There might not be easy solutions in these cases, but educators often jump to threats and isolation as their first line of defense. Researchers have determined that although negative reinforcement may stop a behavior in the short term, it is not an effective or humane way to stop the behavior for the long term (Kohn, 2006).

I admit that it is easy for me to suggest alternatives; I was not the one who was frustrated by the behavior of the student who ran around throwing things at me. Nonetheless, consider some different reactions that the therapist might have had. How do you think the interaction between the occupational therapist and the boy throwing cubes might have changed had the therapist done any of the following?

- Walked over to the student and quietly asked, "What do you need right now?"

- Gave the student a piece of paper and said, "Draw for me what is wrong."

- Calmly asked the student whether he needed a break or a drink of water.

- Asked the student to help clean up the mess.

- Changed the activity entirely and asked the student to help her get ready for the next activity.

- Interpreted the student's behavior and said, "Are you finished?" or "Something seems wrong; can you help me understand what it is?"

Had the occupational therapist responded with any of these reactions, I doubt that the student would have ended up in the time-out room with so much instructional time lost and at a major personal cost to the student and the occupational therapist.

Alfie Kohn, a thoughtful researcher on rewards and punishments, suggested that rewards and punishments work in the short term. But all educators need to ask themselves, "Work to do what?" and "At what cost?" When educators think big about what they want for their students in life, they might think they want all their students to be self-reliant, responsible, socially skilled, caring people. Rewards and punishments produce only temporary compliance. They buy obedience (Kohn, 2006). They do not help anybody develop an intrinsic sense of responsibility. In your own life, think of a task that you do not enjoy doing. For example, I personally dislike taking out the garbage. Now, think for a moment: What if every time I took out the garbage, someone said to me, "Good job taking out the garbage, Julie"? Would that be more motivating? It wouldn't be for me. Sometimes, things people *think* are rewarding are actually not.

All Behavior Communicates Something

It is important to understand that all behavior communicates something. If a student is engaging in challenging behavior, ask yourself, "What might this student be communicating?" Once you have made your best guess at what the student needs, try to meet that student's needs. I watched a paraprofessional do this beautifully. A student, Hayden, was continually tapping a classmate, Sarah, on the back; the tapping seemed to bother Sarah. Instead of assuming that Hayden was trying to be obnoxious or to get attention, the paraprofessional interpreted Hayden's behavior as an attempt to interact with a friend. The paraprofessional whispered to Hayden, "Do you want to move closer and talk with Sarah? One way to start the conversation is to just say 'Hi.'" Hayden moved closer and said "Hi," and the conversation went on from there.

Some useful ways to interpret what a student is communicating include the following:

- *Ask them.* Say, "I see you are doing X; what do you want me to know?" or "It must mean something when you bang your head. What does it mean?"

- *Watch and learn.* Record everything the student does before and after a behavior. Meet with the team and try to determine what the student is attempting to gain from behaving this way.

- *Attribute positive motives.* One of the most important things is to consider what you believe about a particular child. Attribute the best possible motive consistent with the facts (Kohn, 2006). Assume that the student does not have malicious intent; the student probably is trying to get his or her needs met or to communicate something.

I saw this done well in a hallway setting. A girl ran into a teacher in the hall, and the girl's backpack hit the teacher. The teacher bent down and began yelling at the student: "You gotta stop messing around. If you keep this up, I will call your mother." (Trust me, this is not the good part.) A paraprofessional who was walking with the class said, "I do not think she meant to run into you. I saw what happened; she was walking along and talking with her friend. She didn't see you stop, and she didn't mean to run into you."

This situation can be filtered through two different lenses. When you attribute the best possible motive consistent with the facts, you often see things in a positive and, possibly, more accurate light. This positive spin opens the door for more humanistic approaches to behavior. On the other hand, when behavior is interpreted as malicious or mean spirited, it is all too easy to respond in a similar way.

Have you ever been out of control? What do you need when you are out of control? I personally need someone to listen, someone to talk to, someone to not give advice; sometimes, I need a nap or some time away. When students are in the heat of the moment, they often need the most caring, from a calm person. They need a paraprofessional who is safe, calm, and cool and who will gently, calmly provide support.

What students do *not* need in the heat of the moment (or ever, for that matter) is to be ignored; to be yelled at; to be treated with hostility, sarcasm, or public humiliation; or to be forcefully removed from the situation.

Paula Kluth (2005), an expert on behavior management (particularly with students who have autism), offers this advice:

> When a student is kicking, biting, banging her head, or screaming, she is most likely miserable, confused, scared or uncomfortable. The most effective and the most human response at this point is to offer support; to act in a comforting manner, and to help the person relax and feel safe. Teaching can come later. In a crisis, the educator must listen, support and simply be there. (p. 2)

How Are the Other Students Behaving?

When students are supported by paraprofessionals, they invariably are under extra scrutiny. This sometimes leads to behavioral expectations that are more stringent for students with disabilities than for other students. I see this very frequently in classrooms. In one case, I heard a teacher tell a student to sit up tall while working, although two other students in the room were sleeping and one other student was crawling on the floor. Observe how the other students are expected to behave; the student being supported should not be expected to perform at a higher behavioral standard. The cartoon at the beginning of this chapter illustrates this point.

Nothing Personal

As a special educator, I dealt with my fair share of challenging behaviors. The hardest thing for me was not to take anything personally. I had a student who was particularly good at figuring out my buttons and pushing them (or so I thought). But, the best advice I ever heard was to remember that the offensive behavior was "nothing personal." The students I supported invariably had challenging behavior. Whether I was working with them or not, they all were learning how to manage their own behavior. Sometimes, I would tell myself, "It is not personal. Even though this student has just called me a name, it is not about me right now." The challenging behaviors of some students are functions of their disabilities. Just as you would not get angry with a student who was having difficulty walking or reading—because you would assume that this was a function of the student's disability—you should not get angry with students who are struggling to behave. The best, most humane way to respond in these situations is to be helpful and supportive.

Think Like a Parent

Remember that every student is someone's child. When faced with a student's challenging behavior, imagine that you are someone who deeply loves the student. Try to imagine what it would be like if you had watched the child grow and learn from infancy onward; how would you react from that perspective? How might you react if it were your son, daughter, niece, or nephew? If you react from a position of love and acceptance, you are much more likely to respond with kindness and humanity than with punishment and control.

HELPING STUDENTS TO MOVE ON

If a student has just had a significant behavioral outburst, he or she may be embarrassed, tired, or still holding on to negative feelings. It is important to help students move past these experiences. After an outburst, you should let the student know that the crisis is over, validate his or her feelings, and help him or her move on. The phrases listed in Table 8.1 are offered as a guide to help you think about how you can talk to

Table 8.1. How to communicate with students after the behavior occurs

To communicate to a student . . .	You might respond with . . .
That the crisis is over . . .	"You are done with that now."
	"The problem is done."
	Have the student draw the problem, and then have him or her cross it out to signify that the situation has ended.
That you validate this student's feelings . . .	"It is okay to feel that way."
	"I understand that was hard for you."
	"Now it is over."
	"I am sorry that was so hard for you."
	"I can tell you were really frustrated, angry, or upset."
	Draw a picture of the student. Draw thought bubbles over the student's head. Ask the student to help you identify what he or she was thinking and feeling.
It is time to move on . . .	"What do you need now?"
	"What can I help you with to get you back to work?"
	"Do you want to take a rest and prepare to get yourself back together?"
	"Would you prefer to get right back to work?"
	"Draw for me what you need right now."

students to get them beyond emotional crises, but the phrases should not be memorized and repeated. The most important thing is for you to have a calm, loving tone in your voice as you communicate with the student.

Help the student repair any damage. When an adult makes a mistake or loses his or her temper, he or she first needs to repair the damage. Once, while giving a presentation, I made the mistake of using someone in the audience as an example. I did not think it would embarrass that person, but I subsequently learned that it had. I felt awful; I had to repair the damage. I did so by writing a note of apology. Writing an apology note might not be the best way for a student to repair the damage after a behavioral outburst; my point is that you should help the student identify what might help fix the situation and involve him or her in repairing it. The solution should match the problem. For example, if a student knocks books off a shelf during a tantrum, the best solution is to have the student pick up the books. If a student rips up his artwork, the solution might be to have him either tape it together or create a new piece. If a student yells at a peer, a solution might be to have her write an apology note, draw an apology picture, or simply say, "I am sorry." You do not want to make the repair bigger than the problem. The main goal should be to get students back to work in a timely manner.

COMMONLY ASKED QUESTIONS ABOUT BEHAVIORAL SUPPORTS

Q. If a student is not punished, won't he or she simply repeat the behavior?

A. I do not believe in adding on a punishment. In fact, much research has been done on the use of time-outs and punishments. This research suggests that punishments work in the short term but have long-term negative effects on students (Kohn, 2006).

Q. One of my students is not aggressive toward peers—only toward adults. What does that indicate?

A. This type of aggression usually indicates a problem with the type or intensity of support being provided. Students often lash out at paraprofessionals or teachers who make them feel different or uncomfortable because of the support being given. For example, I observed a 12-year-old girl who was being aggressive toward the paraprofessional. I noticed that the paraprofessional was providing intensive support by sitting next to the girl. The paraprofessional was also using a technique called "spidering" (crawling your hand up the back of the student's hair). The student seemed embarrassed and uncomfortable with that type and level of support. When the paraprofessional moved away from the student, the aggression stopped.

Q. I am being asked to provide extensive support and have been told never to leave the student's side. I know this is embarrassing to the student. What should I do?

A. You have to provide the type of support that the team deems appropriate. But, if you think it is not helpful to the student, work with your team and discuss when it might be appropriate to fade your support: What would fading look like for this student? What other types of support can be in place to allow for student success?

Q. Should a student leave the room if he or she is distracting other students?

A. Leaving the room should be the absolute last resort. Try many different stay-put supports. Help the student stay in the environment for all of the reasons mentioned in this chapter. If a student leaves every time he or she makes a noise, that student learns that membership is contingent on being quiet or good. Of course you want to think about other students, but when inclusion is done well, all students understand that a certain student may make noise and that the student is working on that, just as other students may be working on other skills. Most students are surprisingly patient when given the chance and some information.

CONCLUSION

The way educators and paraprofessionals plan for, support, and react to behavior is critical to student success. Remembering that all behavior communicates something and that all people need love and patience will help you be successful when supporting students. Supporting students who have challenging behavior is not easy; therefore, the next and last chapter of this book focuses on caring for yourself so that you can have the energy and ability to provide the best possible care for all students.

NOTES

Supporting You,
Supporting Them

Self-Care

UNFORTUNATELY, THE TEACHER
ASSISTANT'S BURNING QUESTIONS KEPT
SPONTANEOUSLY COMBUSTING BEFORE
THEY COULD BE ANSWERED.

By the time I get home from a day of working with James, I am tired mentally, physically, and emotionally. I can keep it together at work, but when I get home and have my own kids to take care of, I think to myself . . . . Help! . . . I just can't do it all.

—*Jennifer (paraprofessional)*

I find myself a student of the process called *self-care.* I am continually seeking out ways to nurture myself. As a professor, author, consultant, and, most importantly, mother of two small children, I often am in desperate and continual need of self-care. Consequently, I found this chapter the most difficult to write. In one memorable quest for self-care techniques, I helped put my kids to bed, kissed my husband goodbye, and soon found myself standing in the self-help aisle at the local bookstore with a close friend. We read different passages aloud. The books stated I should "become a bonsai tree" or "imagine myself on a glen surrounded by animals while breathing deeply." My first thoughts were, "What is a glen?" and "What kind of animals?" "Are they dangerous?" "Are they rabid?" We began to laugh until other customers looked at us askance. Everyone takes care of himself or herself differently; every person needs to find the way that works best for him or her individually. This chapter does not provide you with a recipe for how to care for yourself; instead, it offers ideas or examples that may help you. Educators who are not rested, healthy, and reasonably content will have difficulty helping their students. Whether you deal with stress by running a marathon or by taking a bath, it is important to focus on what you enjoy and on what works to help you relieve stress and feel healthy and balanced.

The job of a paraprofessional is not easy. Then again, no job worth doing is really easy. You may find the job quite rewarding or quite stressful, or it may vary from day to day. But, one thing is certain: You need to take care of yourself while taking care of others. In essence, you cannot give as fully to others if you are not meeting your own needs. You cannot help others solve problems if you are struggling with your own problems. You also need to set up your own support system. This chapter suggests strategies for problem solving, networking, and self-care. This chapter (and book) concludes with a new job description for paraprofessionals.

PROBLEM SOLVING

Although you have read this book and have several ideas and strategies to handle many different kinds of problems or situations, problems inevitably will arise that you may not feel prepared to handle. When you come across a problem that you are having difficulty solving, consider the following general ideas or suggestions:

- Talk with other teachers in the building.
- Bring the problem to the special education teacher.
- Talk to an occupational therapist.

- Sit down with the question: In what ways might I (fill in the problem here)?
- List all the potential solutions.
- Talk to the student.
- Talk with the principal.
- Talk to a parent.
- Talk with other paraprofessionals.
- Draw the problem.
- Go for a walk—think only of solutions during the walk.
- Talk to your best friend or partner (keep all information about students confidential).

If meeting with others or brainstorming solutions by yourself does not help you discover a new solution, you may need a step-by-step problem-solving process, such as creative problem-solving (CPS).

CREATIVE PROBLEM-SOLVING PROCESS

The CPS process has a long history as a proven method for approaching and solving problems in innovative ways (Davis, 2004; Parnes, 1985, 1988, 1992, 1997). It is a tool that can help you redefine a problem, come up with creative ways to solve the problem, and then take action to solve it. I originally learned this method and used it as a teacher to solve problems with the students whom I supported. I continue to use this method to solve everyday personal and professional problems. Alex Osborn and Sidney Parnes (Osborn, 1993) conducted extensive research on the steps involved when people solve problems. They determined that people typically use a five-step process. Each step is described in the following sections.

Explore the Problem

1. *Fact finding*—Describe what you know or perceive to be true about the challenge. Who? What? When? Where? How? What is true and not true about this problem?

2. *Problem finding*—Clarify the issue. View it in a different way. Finish this sentence: *In what ways might we . . . ?*

Generate Ideas

3. *Idea finding*—Generate as many ideas as possible; defer judgment and reinforcement (do not say things such as "good idea" or "that will not work," because then you would be passing judgment on the idea).

Prepare for Action

4. *Solution finding*—Compare the ideas against some criteria that you create. How will you know whether your solution will work? See Table 9.1 for sample criteria.

5. *Acceptance finding*—Create a step-by-step plan of action.

The following example describes how this process actually worked in solving a specific problem for a paraprofessional.

··········

Tom, a paraprofessional working with Trevor, a first-grade boy, was having a difficult time getting Trevor off the playground at the end of recess. Trevor would run around and hide, and Tom could not reach him or get him to go inside. The end of recess time was becoming a bit like a game of tag, except that Tom definitely did not enjoy chasing Trevor around. Trevor would climb to the top of the slide, and if Tom came up, Trevor would slide down. If Tom went up the slide, Trevor would go down the monkey bars. This was almost humorous to watch unless you were Tom, who felt frustrated and embarrassed. Tom considered the communicative intent of the behavior and decided that Trevor was likely trying to communicate that he did not want to come in from recess. Knowing that information, however, did not help Tom identify what to do to get Trevor inside. He also knew that Trevor had a difficult time with transitions. Tom decided to talk to his team. They sat together and engaged in a CPS process, which is briefly outlined in Table 9.1.

··········

BUILDING A NETWORK OF SUPPORT

If you were all alone in the universe with no one to talk to, no one with which to share the beauty of the stars, to laugh with, to touch, what would be your purpose in life? It is other's life, it is love, which gives your life meaning. This is harmony. We must discover the joy of each other, the joy of challenge, the joy of growth.

—Mitsugi Saotome (1986)

To sustain yourself as a paraprofessional, you need a network of caring support. Do you feel isolated in your workplace? Do you feel that you could use more support? Think of all the people who love you and care about you. Now, consider others at work who also might feel isolated. In your school, classroom, or grade level, create a small team of support.

Table 9.1. The creative problem-solving (CPS) process in action

Stage of CPS process	Examples from Tom and Trevor
1. Fact finding	It doesn't work to wait him out.
	It takes easily 10 minutes to get him off the playground.
	He does not respond to everyone leaving the playground—he continues to play.
	He enjoys playing tag with his friends.
	He has trouble with transitions.
	No one has ever asked him what he needs.
2. Problem finding	In what ways can we help Trevor return from recess promptly and happily?
3. Idea finding	Give him a time out.
	Have him lose minutes off his recess time.
	Give him a timer or watch.
	Have a peer help him in.
	See how long he will play outside before coming in.
	Don't allow him to go outside for recess at all.
	Make a sticker chart.
	Give him extra recess.
4. Solution finding	We want this solution to . . . (example criteria)
	1. Enhance the image of the student among peers.
	2. Promote independence or interdependence.
	3. Appeal to the student.
	4. Increase and promote belonging.
	5. Increase interaction with peers.
	6. Seem logistically feasible.
5. Acceptance finding	The team finally decided on a solution for this problem. What they did was to combine three ideas. They first met with Trevor to ask him what would help (they provided him a menu of ideas); he decided on a timer with peer support. They gave Trevor a watch timer and asked him to identify a peer whom he was to find when the timer went off. When the timer rang (with 2 minutes remaining in recess), the two boys found each other and went to line up together. Problem solved.

Sources: Giangreco, Cloninger, Dennis, and Edelman (2002); Osborn (1993).

Create a Team of Support

One fourth-grade team created a support team by taking turns bringing in breakfast on Friday mornings. They ate together and talked, with no agenda. The conversations were fun and lighthearted, and the team members had time simply to connect with each other. Twice a year, they planned a Saturday morning breakfast to which they invited their families. As they ate together, they got to know more about each other and their loved ones. This helped to create a deeper sense of community for the professionals on the team.

Build a Community with Other Paraprofessionals

A group of paraprofessionals at one school met after school every week and went walking together. Their contract time ended at 3:15 p.m., and they met outside promptly at 3:20 p.m., wearing tennis shoes. They walked a 2-mile path, sharing stories and problems and laughing together along the way. These walks helped them create a network of support, and they also got some exercise and fresh air while they talked.

Another group of paraprofessionals met in the library and formed a book group that alternated between reading work-related books and books selected simply for pleasure. At the beginning of the year, they set their reading list. They organized themselves in such a way that they ended up convincing the principal to purchase the books through their professional development funds. For a useful set of work-related books and articles, see the lists in the Chapter 9 Appendix. These resources should help answer some of your questions, but you undoubtedly will have new questions from day to day. Do not let your questions go unanswered.

Figure out who can help you answer your burning questions. School is a busy place, and, at times, it may seem that no one has time to talk. If you have questions—and you undoubtedly will—write them down and find people who can help you answer them. Consider asking special education teachers, students, general education teachers, other paraprofessionals, principals, therapists, or any other knowledgeable people in the school.

SELF-CARE

Have you ever been on an airplane and heard a flight attendant announce that if there is an emergency, you should place an oxygen mask on your own face before assisting your children? The idea behind that rule is that if the plane crashes, you want to make sure you are available to help the children. If you do not have oxygen, you will not be able to help them. In essence, that is what self-care involves: nurturing yourself outside of work so that you can be helpful and nurturing to the students you support.

Meet Your Own Basic Needs

Maslow (1999) has identified the basic physiological needs of every human; these include oxygen, food, water, and regulated body temperature. Like any other human being, you need to make sure your needs are being met before you can help meet the needs of others. You might have to bring healthy snacks to school to keep yourself fueled for a long day at work. You might bring a water bottle with you so that you can stay hydrated throughout the day. You also might want to have a sweater with you or dress in layers; in many schools, temperatures frequently shift. Maslow's next level of need is safety and love. Surround yourself with loving people so that you feel loved and supported. Lastly, you need to get enough sleep every night. It is much more difficult to be prepared to support students if you are tired and cranky. These needs are at the very core of every person's physical and mental health.

Find an Outlet

Caring for yourself is critical to staying on the job and feeling balanced while doing it. Find ways to sustain yourself while outside of work. Consider physical outlets such as yoga, running, walking, biking, hiking, or swimming. Or, consider spiritual outlets such as meditation, prayer, or yoga to keep yourself spiritually balanced. In the next section, I describe a simple exercise in meditation; try this exercise to help calm you down after a day or to get you prepared before going into work.

An Exercise in Meditation

1. Find a comfortable place where you will not be bothered.
2. Sit with your eyes comfortably closed, and turn your attention inward. Empty your mind of chattering thoughts. Relax.
3. If your mind begins to drift, gently return your focus inward.
4. Sit for as long as you feel comfortable.
5. When you are finished, answer these questions: How do you feel now? Are you energized, thoughtful, contemplative, relaxed, or anxious? Gently acknowledge those feelings and consider trying meditation another time.

Consider intellectual outlets such as playing games, reading, or writing. Or, try more creative outlets such as painting, sculpting, drawing, baking, cooking, scrapbooking, or generally creating something. Consider self-pampering activities such as taking baths, painting your nails, or getting massages. Employing these types of self-care strategies will help you feel balanced, healthy, and calm. See the Chapter 9 Appendix for a list of books on self-care.

As I have mentioned, I consider myself a learner, especially in the area of self-care. When working with children, you need to be constantly learning from them and for them. My hope is that this book will be an impetus for your own learning. When reading this book, try out the strategies, and when you identify a strategy or idea that works, use it again. At the same time, remember that every context, every student, and every minute brings something new. It is important to reflect on when certain ideas or strategies work and how they work. The process is inevitably fluid. At the end of each day, ask yourself the following questions: 1) What worked today? 2) What did not work? 3) What do I want to do differently tomorrow?

I conclude this book with a new job description for paraprofessionals—a call to do things differently. I thank you for reading, and I wish you luck as you help the children you support to reach their full academic and social potential.

HOW TO REALLY SUPPORT A CHILD: A NEW PARAPROFESSIONAL JOB DESCRIPTION

Listen to them. Learn from them. Watch them. Hear them. Support belonging. Be there, but give them space. Let them learn. Let them fail sometimes. Encourage independence. Love them. Always speak kindly. Ask, "What do you need?" Stop yelling. Be safe. Handle them with care. Be respectful. Be gentle. Be trustworthy. Remember, this is a person first. If they are loud, be quiet. Encourage interdependence. If they are sad, wipe their tears. Help students connect. Assume friendship is possible. Allow students to create together, laugh together, and have fun together. Assume competence always. Attribute the best possible motive consistent with the facts. Spark curiosity. Do not control. When students are happy, step back. Allow choice. Relax. Be a learner yourself. Ask, "How can I best help you?" Share positive stories with students' parents. Set students up to be successful. When they have difficulties, kindly redirect. Breathe. Step back. Speak softly. Encourage softly. Redirect softly. Follow their lead. Lead by loving. Give them space. Watch them thrive.

Chapter 9 Appendix

Great Book Club Books for Paraprofessionals

Doyle, M.B. (2008). *The paraprofessional's guide to the inclusive classroom: Working as a team* (3rd ed.). Baltimore: Paul H. Brookes Publishing Co.

Giangreco, M.F., & Doyle, M.B. (Eds.). (2007). *Quick-guides to inclusion: Ideas for educating students with disabilities* (2nd ed.). Baltimore: Paul H. Brookes Publishing Co.

Hammeken, P.A. (1996). *Inclusion: An essential guide for the paraprofessional.* Minnetonka, MN: Peytral Publications.

Kluth, P. (2003). *"You're going to love this kid!": Teaching students with autism in the inclusive classroom.* Baltimore: Paul H. Brookes Publishing Co.

Kluth, P., & Schwarz, P. (2008). *"Just give him the whale!": 20 ways to use fascinations, areas of expertise, and strengths to support students with autism.* Baltimore: Paul H. Brookes Publishing Co.

Kohn, A. (2006). *Beyond discipline: From compliance to community* (10th anniversary ed.). Alexandria, VA: Association for Supervision and Curriculum Development.

Schwartz, P., & Kluth, P. (2008). *You're welcome: 30 innovative ideas for the inclusive classroom.* Portsmouth, NH: Heinemann.

Tashie, C., Shapiro-Barnard, S., & Rossetti, Z. (2006). *Seeing the charade: What people need to do and undo to make friendships happen.* Nottingham, England: Inclusive Solutions.

Great Articles for Paraprofessionals

Black, S. (2002, May). Not just helping hands. *American School Board Journal, 189*(5), 42–44.

Carroll, D. (2001, November/December). Considering paraeducator training, roles, and responsibilities. *TEACHING Exceptional Children, 34*(2), 60–64.

Causton-Theoharis, J., Giangreco, M., Doyle, M.B., & Vadasy, P. (2007). Paraprofessionals: The sous-chefs of literacy instruction. *TEACHING Exceptional Children, 40*(1), 56–63.

Causton-Theoharis, J., & Malmgren, K. (2005). Building bridges: Strategies to help paraprofessionals promote peer interactions. *TEACHING Exceptional Children, 37*(6), 18–24.

Giangreco, M.F. (2003). Working with paraprofessionals. *Educational Leadership, 61*(2), 50–53.

Giangreco, M.F., & Doyle, M.B. (2002). Students with disabilities and paraprofessional supports: Benefits, balance, and band-aids. *Focus on Exceptional Children, 34*(7), 1–12.

Giangreco, M.F., Yuan, S., McKenzie, B., Cameron, P., & Fialka, J. (2005). "Be careful what you wish for . . . ": Five reasons to be concerned about the assignment of individual paraprofessionals. *TEACHING Exceptional Children, 37*(5), 28–34.

Jolly, A., & Evans, S. (2005). Teacher assistants move to the front of the class: Job-embedded learning pays off in student achievement. *Journal of Staff Development, 26*(3), 8–13.

Keller, C.L., Bucholz, J., & Brady, M.P. (2007). Yes, I can! Empowering paraprofessionals to teach learning strategies. *TEACHING Exceptional Children, 39*(3), 18–23.

Mueller, P.H. (2002). The paraeducator paradox. *Exceptional Parent, 32*(9), 64–67.

Patterson, K.B. (2006). Roles and responsibilities of paraprofessionals: In their own words. *TEACHING Exceptional Children Plus, 2*(5), Article 1.

Riggs, C.G. (2001, January/February). Ask the paraprofessionals: What are your training needs? *TEACHING Exceptional Children, 33*(3), 78–83.

Riggs, C.G. (2004, May/June). To teachers: What paraeducators want you to know. *TEACHING Exceptional Children, 36*(5), 8–12.

Self-Care Books

Byrne, R. (2006). *The secret.* New York: Atria Books/Beyond Words.

Carlson, R. (1998). *Don't sweat the small stuff at work: Simple ways to minimize stress and conflict while bringing out the best in yourself and others.* New York: Hyperion.

Covey, S.R. (2004). *The 7 habits of highly effective people: Powerful lessons in personal change* (15th Anniv. Ed.). New York: Free Press.

Fontana, D. (1999). *Learn to meditate: A practical guide to self-discovery.* London: Duncan Baird.

Hoff, B. (1983). *The tao of Pooh.* New York: Penguin.

Moran, V. (1999). *Creating a charmed life: Sensible, spiritual secrets every busy woman should know.* New York: HarperOne.

Palmer, P. (1999). *Let your life speak: Listening to the voice of vocation.* San Francisco: Jossey-Bass.

Palmer, P. (2004). *A hidden wholeness: The journey towards the undivided life.* San Francisco: Jossey-Bass.

Reynolds, S. (2005). *Better than chocolate.* Berkeley, CA: Ten Speed Press.

SARK. (1991). *A creative companion: How to free your creative spirit.* New York: Fireside.

SARK. (1994). *Living juicy: Daily morsels for your creative soul.* New York: Fireside.

SARK. (1997). *Succulent wild women.* New York: Fireside.

SARK. (2005). *Make your creative dreams real: A plan for procrastinators, perfectionists, busy people, and people who would really rather sleep all day.* New York: Fireside.

Topchik, G. (2001). *Managing workplace negativity.* New York: AMACOM.

Wheatley, M.J. (2002). *Turning to one another: Simple conversation to restore hope in the future.* San Francisco: Berrett-Koehler Press.

References

American Psychiatric Association. (2000). *Diagnostic and statistical manual of mental disorders, fourth edition, text revision (DSM-IV-TR)*. Washington, DC: Author.

Armstrong, T. (2000a). *In their own way: Discovering and encouraging your child's multiple intelligences*. New York: Penguin Putnam.

Armstrong, T. (2000b). *Multiple intelligences in the classroom*. Alexandria, VA: Association for Supervision and Curriculum Development.

Ashby, C.E. (2008). *"Cast into a cold pool": Inclusion and access in middle school for students with labels of mental retardation and autism*. Unpublished doctoral dissertation, Syracuse University, Syracuse, NY.

Biklen, D. (2005). *Autism and the myth of the person alone* (pp. 80–82). New York: New York University Press.

Biklen, D., & Burke, J. (2006). Presuming competence. *Equity & Excellence in Education, 39*, 166–175.

Black, S. (2002, May). Not just helping hands. *American School Board Journal, 189*(5), 42–44.

Blatt, B. (1987). *The conquest of mental retardation*. Austin, TX: PRO-ED.

Bonner Foundation. (2008). Conflict resolution: Steps for handling interpersonal dynamics. In *Bonner civic engagement training modules*. Retrieved June 19, 2008, from http://www.bonner.org/resources/modules/home.htm

Broer, S.M., Doyle, M.B., & Giangreco, M.F. (2005). Perspectives of students with disabilities of their experiences with paraprofessional support. *Exceptional Children, 71*(4), 415–430.

Brown, L., Farrington, K., Knight, T., Ross, C., & Ziegler, M. (1999). Fewer paraprofessionals and more teachers and therapists in educational programs for students with significant disabilities. *The Journal of the Association for Persons with Severe Handicaps, 24*(4), 250–253.

Byrne, R. (2006). *The secret*. New York: Atria Books/Beyond Words.

Callahan, C. (2008). *Advice about being an LD student*. Retrieved June 15, 2008, from http://www.ldonline.org/firstperson/8550

Carlson, R. (1998). *Don't sweat the small stuff at work: Simple ways to minimize stress and conflict while bringing out the best in yourself and others*. New York: Hyperion.

Carr, E.G., Dunlap, G., Horner, R.H., Koegel, R.L., Turnbull, A., Sailor, W., et al. (2002). Positive behavior support: Evolution of an applied science. *Journal of Positive Behavior Interventions, 4*(1), 4–16.

Carroll, D. (2001, November/December). Considering paraeducator training, roles, and responsibilities. *TEACHING Exceptional Children, 34*(2), 60–64.

Casey, K., & Vanceburg, M. (1996). *A promise of a new day: A book of daily meditations*. Center City, MN: Hazelden.

Causton-Theoharis, J., Giangreco, M., Doyle, M.B., & Vadasy, P. (2007). Paraprofessionals: The sous chefs of literacy instruction. *TEACHING Exceptional Children, 40*(1), 56–63.

Causton-Theoharis, J., & Malmgren, K. (2005). Building bridges: Strategies to help paraprofessionals promote peer interactions. *TEACHING Exceptional Children, 37*(6), 18–24.

Causton-Theoharis, J., & Theoharis, G. (2008, September). Creating inclusive schools for all students. *The School Administrator, 65*(8), 24–30.

Causton-Theoharis, J., Theoharis, G., Bull, T., & Cosier, M. (2008, March). *Changing the flow of the river: Inclusive school reform*. Paper presented at the American Educational Research Association Annual Meeting, New York.

Covey, S.R. (2004). *The 7 habits of highly effective people: Powerful lessons in personal change* (15th Anniv. Ed.). New York: Free Press.

Davis, G. (2004). *Creativity is forever* (5th ed.). Dubuque, IA: Kendall Hunt Publishing.

Donnellan, A. (1984). The criterion of the least dangerous assumption. *Behavioral Disorders, 9,* 141–150.

Doyle, M.B. (2008). *The paraprofessional's guide to the inclusive classroom: Working as a team* (3rd ed.). Baltimore: Paul H. Brookes Publishing Co.

Education for All Handicapped Children Act of 1975, PL 94-142, 20 U.S.C. §§ 1400 *et seq.*

FAS Community Resource Center. (2008). *Information about fetal alcohol syndrome (FAS) and fetal alcohol spectrum disorders (FASD).* Retrieved March 25, 2008, from http://www.come-over.to/FASCRC

Fontana, D. (1999). *Learn to meditate: A practical guide to self-discovery.* London: Duncan Baird.

French, N.K. (1998). Working together: Resource teachers and paraeducators. *Remedial and Special Education, 19*(6), 357–368.

Friend, M., & Reising, M. (1993, Summer). Co-teaching: An overview of the past, a glimpse at the present, and considerations for the future. *Preventing School Failure, 37*(4), 6–10.

Gabel, A. (2006). Stop asking me if I need help. In E.B. Keefe, V.M. Moore, & F.R. Duff (Eds.), *Listening to the experts: Students with disabilities speak out* (pp. 35–40). Baltimore: Paul H. Brookes Publishing Co.

Gardner, H. (1993). *Frames of mind: A theory of multiple intelligences.* New York: Basic Books.

Giangreco, M.F. (2003). Working with paraprofessionals. *Educational Leadership, 61*(2), 50–53.

Giangreco, M.F. (2007). *Absurdities and realities of special education: The complete digital set.* [CD]. Thousands Oaks, CA: Crown Press.

Giangreco, M.F., Broer, S.M., & Edelman, S.W. (2002). "That was then, this is now!" Paraprofessional supports for students with disabilities in general education classrooms. *Exceptionality, 10*(1), 47–64.

Giangreco, M.F., Cloninger, C.J., Dennis, R., & Edelman, S.W. (2002). Problem-solving methods to facilitate inclusive education. In J.S. Thousand, R.A. Villa & A.I. Nevin (Eds.), *Creativity and collaborative learning: The practical guide to empowering students, teachers, and families* (2nd ed., pp. 111–134). Baltimore: Paul H. Brookes Publishing Co.

Giangreco, M.F., & Doyle, M.B. (2002). Students with disabilities and paraprofessional supports: Benefits, balance, and band-aids. *Focus on Exceptional Children, 34*(7), 1–12.

Giangreco, M.F., & Doyle, M.B. (Eds.). (2007). *Quick-guides to inclusion: Ideas for educating students with disabilities* (2nd ed.). Baltimore: Paul H. Brookes Publishing Co.

Giangreco, M.F., Edelman, S.W., Luiselli, E.T., & MacFarland, S.Z. (1997). Helping or hovering: The effects of paraprofessional proximity on students with disabilities. *Exceptional Children, 64*(1), 7–18.

Giangreco, M.F., Yuan, S., McKenzie, B., Cameron, P., & Fialka, J. (2005). "Be careful what you wish for . . .": Five reasons to be concerned about the assignment of individual paraprofessionals. *TEACHING Exceptional Children, 37*(5), 28–34.

Hammeken, P.A. (1996). *Inclusion: An essential guide for the paraprofessional.* Minnetonka, MN: Peytral Publications.

Hoff, B. (1983). *The tao of Pooh.* New York: Penguin.

Huefner, D.S. (2000). *Getting comfortable with special education law: A framework for working with children with disabilities.* Norwood, MA: Christopher-Gordon.

Individuals with Disabilities Education Improvement Act (IDEA) of 2004, PL 108-446, 20 U.S.C. §§ 1400 *et seq.*

Institut Pasteur. (n.d.). *Louis Pasteur's biography.* Retrieved September 9, 2008, from http://www.pasteur.fr/pasteur/histoire/histoireUS/BioPasteur.html

Janney, R., & Snell, M.E. (2008). *Teachers' guides to inclusive practices: Behavioral support* (2nd ed.). Baltimore: Paul H. Brookes Publishing Co.

Jolly, A., & Evans, S. (2005). Teacher assistants move to the front of the class: Job-embedded learning pays off in student achievement. *Journal of Staff Development, 26*(3), 8–13.

Jones, R.C. (1998–2006). *Strategies for reading comprehension: Clock buddies.* Retrieved September 26, 2008, from http://www.readingquest.org/strat/clock_buddies.html

Keller, C.L., Bucholz, J., & Brady, M.P. (2007). Yes, I can! Empowering paraprofessionals to teach learning strategies. *TEACHING Exceptional Children, 39*(3), 18–23.

Keller, H. (1903). *The story of my life.* New York: Doubleday, Page, & Co.

Kliewer, C., & Biklen, D. (1996). Labeling: Who wants to be called retarded? In W. Stainback & S. Stainback (Eds.), *Controversial issues confronting special education: Divergent perspectives* (2nd ed., pp. 83–111). Boston: Allyn & Bacon.

Kluth, P. (2003). *"You're going to love this kid!": Teaching students with autism in the inclusive classroom.* Baltimore: Paul H. Brookes Publishing Co.

Kluth, P. (2005). Calm in crisis. Adapted from P. Kluth (2003). *"You're going to love this kid!": Teaching students with autism in the inclusive classroom.* Baltimore: Paul H. Brookes Publishing Co. Retrieved October 15, 2008, from http://www.paulakluth.com/articles/calmincrisis.html

Kluth, P., & Schwarz, P. (2008). *"Just give him the whale!": 20 ways to use fascinations, areas of expertise, and strengths to support students with autism.* Baltimore: Paul H. Brookes Publishing Co.

Knoster, T.P. (2008). *The teacher's pocket guide for effective classroom management.* Baltimore: Paul H. Brookes Publishing Co.

Kohn, A. (2006). *Beyond discipline: From compliance to community* (10th anniversary ed.). Alexandria, VA: Association for Supervision and Curriculum Development.

Kornhaber, M., Fierros, E., & Veenema, S. (2004). *Multiple intelligences: Best ideas from research and practice.* Boston: Pearson Education.

Kunc, N. (1992). The need to belong: Rediscovering Maslow's hierarchy of needs. In R. Villa, J. Thousand, W. Stainback, & S. Stainback (Eds.), *Restructuring for caring and effective education* (pp. 21–40). Baltimore: Paul H. Brookes Publishing Co.

Latham, G.I. (1999). *Parenting with love: Making a difference in a day.* Logan, UT: P&T Ink.

Living with ADD. (2004). *Brian.* Retrieved September 19, 2008, from http://www.livingwithadd.com/stories/2004/bri.shtml

Lovett, H. (1996). *Learning to listen: Positive approaches and people with difficult behavior.* Baltimore: Paul H. Brookes Publishing Co.

Madison Public Schools. (2007). *Paraprofessional job description.* Madison, WI: Author.

Malmgren, K.W., & Causton-Theoharis, J.N. (2006). Boy in the bubble: Effects of paraprofessional proximity and other pedagogical decisions on the interactions of a student with behavioral disorders. *Journal of Research in Childhood Education, 20*(4), 301–312.

Maslow, A.H. (1999). *Toward a psychology of being.* New York: John Wiley & Sons.

Mavis. (2007, October 7). *Living in the hearing and deaf worlds.* Retrieved June 19, 2008, from http://www.raisingdeafkids.org/meet/deaf/mavis/worlds.php

McLeskey, J., & Waldron, N. (2006). Comprehensive school reform and inclusive schools: Improving schools for all students. *Theory into Practice, 45*(3), 269–278.

Molton, K. (2000). *Dispelling some myths about autism.* Retrieved April 15, 2009, from http://www.nas.org.uk/nas/jsp/polopoly.jsp?d=120&a=2202

Moran, V. (1999). *Creating a charmed life: Sensible, spiritual secrets every busy woman should know.* New York: HarperOne.

Mueller, P.H. (2002). The paraeducator paradox. *Exceptional Parent, 32*(9), 64–67.

Murawski, W.W., & Dieker, L.A. (2004). Tips and strategies for co-teaching at the secondary level. *TEACHING Exceptional Children, 36*(5), 52–58.

No Child Left Behind Act of 2001, PL 107-110, 115 Stat. 1425, 20 U.S.C. §§ 6301 *et seq.*

OrganizedWisdom. (2008). *Borderline personality disorder.* Retrieved September, 19, 2008, from http://organizedwisdom.com/helpbar/index.html?return=http://organizedwisdom.com/Antisocial_Personality_Disorder_Blogs_and_Personal_Stories&url=www.angelfire.com/home/bphoenix1/antis.html

Orwell, G. (1981). Politics and English language. In *A collection of essays* (pp. 156–170). Orlando, FL: Harvest.

Osborn, A.F. (1993). *Applied imagination: Principles and procedures of creative problem-solving* (3rd rev. ed.). Buffalo, NY: Creative Education Foundation Press. (Original work published 1953)

Palmer, P. (1999). *Let your life speak: Listening to the voice of vocation.* San Francisco: Jossey-Bass.

Palmer, P. (2004). *A hidden wholeness: The journey towards the undivided life.* San Francisco: Jossey-Bass.

Parker, K. (2008). *Meet RhapsodyBlue.* Retrieved September 19, 2008, from http://www.angelfire.com/country/rhapsodyblue22/page2.html

Parnes, S.J. (1985). *A facilitating style of leadership.* Buffalo, NY: Bearly.

Parnes, S.J. (1988). *Visionizing: State-of-the-art processes for encouraging innovative excellence.* East Aurora, NY: D.O.K. Publishing.

Parnes, S.J. (Ed.). (1992). *Source book for creative problem solving: A fifty-year digest of proven innovation processes.* Buffalo, NY: Creative Education Foundation Press.

Parnes, S.J. (1997). *Optimize the magic of your mind.* Buffalo, NY: Creative Education Foundation Press.

Patterson, K.B. (2006). Roles and responsibilities of paraprofessionals: In their own words. *TEACHING Exceptional Children Plus, 2*(5), Article 1. Retrieved May 29, 2008, from escholarship.bc.edu/cgi/viewcontent.cgi?article=1189&context=education/tecplus/iss2/vol5/art1

Paul-Brown, D., & Diggs, M.C. (1993, Winter). Recognizing and treating speech and language disabilities. *American Rehabilitation.* Retrieved December 14, 2008, from http://findarticles.com/p/articles/mi_m0842/is_/ai_15538210

PEAK Parent Center. (n.d.). *Accommodations and modifications fact sheet.* Retrieved September 12, 2008, from http://www.peatc.org/peakaccom.htm

Peterson, J.M., & Hittie, M.M. (2002). *Inclusive teaching: Creating effective schools for all learners.* Boston: Allyn & Bacon.

Pitonyak, D. (2007). *The importance of belonging.* Retrieved September 25, 2008, from http://www.dimagine.com/page5.html

Reynolds, S. (2005). *Better than chocolate.* Berkeley, CA: Ten Speed Press.

Riggs, C.G. (2001, January/February). Ask the paraprofessionals: What are your training needs? *TEACHING Exceptional Children, 33*(3), 78–83.

Riggs, C.G. (2004, May/June). To teachers: What paraeducators want you to know. *TEACHING Exceptional Children, 36*(5), 8–12.

Rubin, S. (2003, December). *Making dreams come true.* Paper presented at the annual conference of TASH, Chicago.

Saotome, M. (1986). The dojo: Spiritual oasis. In *Aikido and the harmony of nature* (pp. 246–248). Boulogne, France: SEDIREP.

SARK. (1991). *A creative companion: How to free your creative spirit.* New York: Fireside.

SARK. (1994). *Living juicy: Daily morsels for your creative soul.* New York: Fireside.

SARK. (1997). *Succulent wild women.* New York: Fireside.

SARK. (2005). *Make your creative dreams real: A plan for procrastinators, perfectionists, busy people, and people who would really rather sleep all day.* New York: Fireside.

Schalock, R.L., & Braddock, D.L. (2002). *Out of the darkness and into the light: Nebraska's experience with mental retardation.* Washington DC: American Association on Mental Retardation.

Schwarz, P., & Kluth, P. (2008). *You're welcome: 30 innovative ideas for the inclusive classroom.* Portsmouth, NH: Heinemann.

Snow, K. (2008). *To ensure inclusion, freedom, and respect for all, it's time to embrace people first language.* Retrieved June 19, 2008, from http://www.disabilityisnatural.com/peoplefirstlanguage.htm

Strully, J.L., & Strully, C. (1996). Friendships as an educational goal: What we have learned and where we are headed. In S. Stainback & W. Stainback (Eds.), *Inclusion: A guide for educators* (pp. 141–154). Baltimore: Paul H. Brookes Publishing Co.

Tashie, C., Shapiro-Barnard, S., & Rossetti, Z. (2006). *Seeing the charade: What people need to do and undo to make friendships happen.* Nottingham, UK: Inclusive Solutions.

Taylor, R.L., Smiley, L.R., & Richards, S.B. (2009). *Exceptional students: Preparing teaching for the 21st century.* New York: McGraw-Hill.

Topchik, G. (2001). *Managing workplace negativity.* New York: AMACOM.

Turnbull, H.R., Turnbull, A.R., Shank, M., & Smith, S.J. (2004). *Exceptional lives: Special education in today's schools* (4th ed.). Upper Saddle River, NJ: Merrill/Prentice Hall.

Udvari-Solner, A. (1997). Inclusive education. In C.A. Grant & G. Ladson-Billings (Eds.), *Dictionary of multicultural education* (pp. 141–144). Phoenix, AZ: Oryx Press.

U.S. Department of Education. (2000, July). Contents of the IEP. In *A guide to the individualized education program.* Washington, DC: Author.

U.S. Department of Education. (2004). *Twenty-fourth annual report to Congress on the implementation of the Individuals with Disabilities Education Act.* Washington DC: Author.

U.S. Department of Education. (2007, September). *Twenty-seventh annual report to Congress on the implementation of the Individuals with Disabilities Education Act, 2005* (Vol. 1). Washington, DC: Author.

Weil, S. (2001). *The need for roots.* London: Routledge

Wheatley, M.J. (2002). *Turning to one another: Simple conversation to restore hope in the future.* San Francisco: Berrett-Koehler Press.

Will, M. (1986). *Educating students with learning problems: A shared responsibility.* Washington, DC: U.S. Department of Education, Office of Special Education and Rehabilitative Service.

Williams, R. (Presenter). (2008, August 24). Hearing impairment: A personal story [Radio broadcast]. In B. Seega (Producer), *Ockham's razor.* Transcript retrieved September 19, 2008, from http://www.abc.net.au/rn/ockhamsrazor/stories/2008/2342555.htm

Index

Page numbers followed by *f* indicate figures; those followed by *t* indicate tables.

Academic supports, 5, 75–92
  ask the student, 79
  assistive technology, 89–90
  break tasks into small steps, 79–80
  change materials, 81
  common activities and supports, 85–89*t*
  commonly asked questions, 90, 92
  extend time on tasks, 80
  focus on strengths, 79
  keep expectations high, 79
  limited information on a page, 80
  literacy support, 85
  make things concrete, 80–81
  offer, don't just give support, 80
  peer support, 82
  preteach, 82
  soft voice, 80
  teach organization skills, 81
  timer use, 81–82
  use movement, 82
Acceptance finding, step in creative problem
  solving (CPS), 114
Accommodations, 76–78
  examples, 78
  for special education, 12
Adaptations, 76–78
ADD/ADHD, *see* Attention deficit
  disorder/Attention-deficit/hyperactivity
  disorder
Age-appropriate language, 56–57
Articles for paraprofessionals, 119–120
Assistive technology, 89–90
  device, 89
  service, 89
  web sites and resources, 93
Attention deficit disorder and/or
  attention-deficit/hyperactivity disorder
  (ADD/ADHD), 16, 21
Autism, category of disability, 17
Autonomy, for students, 102

Behavior
  communication through, 105–106
  other students, 106
Behavioral intervention plan (BIP), 16
Behavioral support, 5, 95–110
  commonly asked questions, 108–109
  tasks, 7, 8*t*
Belonging, 28–29

Bodily kinesthetic intelligence, 55*t*
Bonner Foundation, steps in conflict
  resolution, 47
Books for paraprofessionals, 119
Bridging students with peers, 67–69

Case manager, 9
CBI, *see* Community-based instruction
Challenging behavior
  helping students move on, 107–108, 108t
  nothing personal, 106
  think like a parent, 107
  typical response, 97
  weathering the storm, 103–105
Clerical assistant, 5
Clerical tasks, 7, 8*t*
Clock Buddies sheet, 71*f*
Cognitive disabilities, 20
Collaborating with others, 39–50
  commonly asked questions, 49
Common activities and supports, 85–89*t*
Communication
  students' need for, 102–103
  through behavior, 105–106
Communications notebook, alternative to
  meeting, 48
Community-based classrooms, 7
Community-based instruction (CBI), 16
Community building, in inclusive classrooms,
  31–32
Confidentiality, in team teaching, 48
Conflict resolution, 47
Cosupport, 45–46, 46*t*
Creative problem-solving (CPS) process,
  113–114, 115*t*
Cycle of support, 77*f*

Deafblindness, category of disability, 18
Deafness, category of disability, 18
Differentiation, in inclusive classrooms, 32
Disability
  federally recognized categories, 16–24,
    24*f*
  in general education settings, 3, 5
  labels, 15
  social construction of, 14–15
  understanding a student's label, 14
Down syndrome (DS), 16

E-mail, alternative to meeting, 48
Education for All Handicapped Children Act of 1975 (PL 94-142), 3, 30
Emotional behavioral disturbance (EBD), 16
Emotional disturbance (ED), 16
  category of disability, 18–19
Engaging instruction, in inclusive classrooms, 32
Environment, for promotion of positive behavior, 101
Explore the problem, step in creative problem solving (CPS), 113
Extended school year (ESY), 16

Facilitating relationships, 67–69
  before and after school, 69
  free or choice time, 70
  hallway interactions, 69
  lunchtime, 69–70
  selection of partners, 70–71
Fading assistance, 66–67
Family, role in teaching team, 42
Free appropriate public education (FAPE), 16, 30
Friendships, importance of, 62–63
Functional behavioral assessment (FBA), 16

Gender differences, special education population, 13
General educator, role in teaching team, 41–42
Generate ideas, step in creative problem solving (CPS), 113
Gentle and respectful support, 64

Hearing impaired, 16
Hearing impairment, category of disability, 19
Hiding in full view, art of paraprofessional support, 64
How to really support a child, 118

IDEA, see Individuals with Disabilities Education Improvement Act of 2004
IEPs, see Individualized education programs
Impairment-driven descriptions, 52–53
Inclusion/exclusion feelings, 29t
Inclusive classrooms, 6, 13
  indicators, 31–32
  removal of student, 65
Inclusive education, 13, 27–38
  commonly asked questions, 33–37
  definitions, 31
  history of, 29–30
  natural proportions, 31
Independence and interdependence, encouragement, 65
Individualized education programs (IEPs), 5, 16
example, 35f
  how to read, 34t
  learning about your student, 24–25

role of paraprofessional and, 6
special educator design of, 41
what I need to know, 32–36
what it includes, 33
Individuals with Disabilities Education Improvement Act (IDEA) of 2004 (PL 108-446), 3, 16, 30
  assistive technology, 89
  definition of a student with a disability, 13
  definition of paraprofessional, 4
  family role in teaching team, 42
  legal definition of special education, 12
  modifications, 12
  who receives services, 13–14
Instructional tasks, 7, 8t
Intellectual disabilities, 20
Intelligence, defined by educators, 54–55
Interdependence, students' need for, 102
Interpersonal intelligence, 55t
Intrapersonal intelligence, 55t
IQ testing, 54

Job description, 9

Kids do not leave to learn, in inclusive classrooms, 32

Labels
  avoiding, 57–58
  disability categories, 14–16
Learning differently, versus learning disabled, 53
Learning facilitator, paraprofessional as, 4–5
Least dangerous assumption, 56
Least restrictive environment (LRE), 13, 16, 30
Lesson plan sharing, alternative to team meetings, 48
Literacy support, 85
Logical mathematical intelligence, 55t
Logistics, in teaching team, 44–45
LRE, see Least restrictive environment

Mailbox, alternative to meeting, 48
Mainstreaming, 3
  see also Inclusive education
Materials, offer choices, 81
Mental retardation (MR), 16
  category of disability, 19–20
Modifications, 76–78
  content-specific strategies, 82–89, 83–84t
  examples, 78
  general strategies, 78–2
  for special education, 12
Movement, use in academic support, 82
Multiple disabilities, category of disability, 20
Multiple Intelligence theory, 53
Multiple intelligences, 54–55, 55t
Musical intelligence, 55t

Naturalistic intelligence, 55*t*
Network of support, for self-care, 114
New material, role of paraprofessional, 9
No Child Left Behind Act (NCLB) of 2001
  (PL 107-110)
  definition of paraprofessional, 4
  supervision of paraprofessionals, 76

Occupational therapist, 16
  role in teaching team, 42
One teach–one observe, 45–46
One teach–one support, 45–46
Organizational skills, for everyone, 81
Orthopedic impairments, 16
  category of disability, 20
Other health impairments, category of
  disability, 21

Paraprofessionals
  benefits of, 6
  books and articles for, 119–120
  building continuity with others, 116
  from caregiver to learning facilitator, 4–5
  changes in title over time, 5
  confidentiality considerations, 48
  definitions, 4
  expected tasks and responsibilities, 7, 8*t*
  fading assistance, 66–67
  history of, 3
  a new job description, 118
  positioning during instruction, 64–65
  providing social support, 61–74
  qualifications, 4
  role as bridge, 67–69
  role in teaching team, 41
  roles and responsibilities, 5–6, 8–9
  use of IEPs, 33
  to whom do I report?, 8–9
  work settings, 6–7
Parent volunteer, use for team meeting
  time, 48
PBS, *see* Positive behavioral support
PEAK Parent Center, 77
Peer support, 65
  encouragement of, 82
Person-first language, 57–58, 58*t*
Personal care tasks, 7, 8*t*
Philosophy, in teaching team, 44
Physical support, 5
Physical therapist, 16
  role in teaching team, 42
PL 94-142, *see* Education for All Handicapped
  Children Act of 1975
PL 108-446, *see* Individuals with Disabilities
  Education Improvement Act (IDEA) of 2004
PL 107-110, *see* No Child Left Behind Act
  (NCLB) of 2001
Planning or preparation tasks, 7, 8*t*
Pleasure and joy, students' need for, 102

Positive behavioral support (PBS), 16, 97–98
  environment, 101
Poverty, special education population, 14
Prepare for action, step in creative problem
  solving (CPS), 114
Presume competence, 56
Proactive behavioral management, 98–103
Problem solving, 112–113
Program assistant, 5
Proofread notes to parents, alternative to team
  meetings, 48
Psychologist, role in teaching team, 43

Race/ethnicity, special education
  population, 14
Rapport building, 99–101
Relationship building, 98–99
Relationships and interdependence, needs
  of students, 102
Removal of student from classroom, 65
Resource rooms, 6–7
Rethinking students, 51–60

Safety and trust, students' need for, 102
Self-care, 111–118
  books for, 120
  exercise in meditation, 116–117
  find an outlet, 116
  meet your own basic needs, 116
Self-contained classrooms, 7
Service coordinator, 9
SLD, *see* Specific learning disability
Small-group discussion, role of
  paraprofessional, 9
Social interaction, teaching the rules, 72
Social supports, 5, 61–74
  commonly asked questions, 72–73
  five ways for natural support, 64–67
  instructional time, 71–72
  types, 66*t*
  unstructured time, 69–71
Social worker, role in teaching team, 43
Solution finding, step in creative problem
  solving (CPS), 114
Spatial intelligence, 55*t*
Special education, 11–26
  acronyms, 16
  commonly asked questions, 24–25
  definition, 12–13
  a service, not a place, 13
  terminology, 16
  who receives services, 13–14
Special educator, role in teaching team, 41
Specials time, team meetings, 48
Specific learning disability (SLD), 16
  category of disability, 21–22
Speech and language, 16
category of disability, 22
speech pathologist, 42

Speech and language therapist, role in teaching team, 42
Speech-language pathologist, 16
Station facilitation, 45–46
Sticky note, 21 ways to use, 89, 90*f*
Strengths
   focus when providing support, 79
   reframing conceptions of students, 53–54
Student descriptions, 52–53, 54*t*
   commonly asked questions, 59
Students' needs, 101–103
   a plan for each student, 103
Supervision tasks, 7, 8*t*
Supplementary aids and services, 30–31
Support team, creation of, 116

Tasks
   break into small steps, 79–80
   extend time, 80
Teacher aide, 5
Teaching aide, 5
Teaching assistant, 5
Team teaching
   commonly asked questions, 49
   conflict, 46–47
   cosupporting arrangements, 45–46
   ethical considerations, 48

   guiding questions, 44–45
   in inclusive classrooms, 31
   making time to communicate, 47–48
   roles and responsibilities, 40–43
   using another team to create time, 48
   working together, 43–44
Traumatic brain injury (TBI), 16
   category of disability, 22–23

Unstructured time, providing support during, 69–71

Velcro phenomenon, 63–64
Verbal/linguistic intelligence, 55*t*
Video or independent work time, use for team meeting time, 47
Vision teacher/audiologist, role in teaching team, 43
Visual impairment, 16
Visual impairment (including blindness), category of disability, 23

Word window, 80
Work styles, in teaching team, 44
Written plans, for paraprofessionals, 9